STEADFAST

LIZZIE
ARMITSTEAD

STEADFAST
MY STORY

WITH WILLIAM FOTHERINGHAM

BLINK
bringing you closer

Published by Blink Publishing
3.08, The Plaza,
535 Kings Road,
Chelsea Harbour,
London, SW10 0SZ

www.blinkpublishing.co.uk

facebook.com/blinkpublishing
twitter.com/blinkpublishing

HB – 978-1-91127-425-4
TPB – 978-1-91127-432-2
Ebook – 978-1-91127-426-1

A CIP catalogue of this book is available from the British Library.

Printed and bound by Clays Ltd, St Ives plc

1 3 5 7 9 10 8 6 4 2

Papers used by Blink Publishing are natural, recyclable products made from wood grown in sustainable forests. The manufacturing processes conform to the environmental regulations of the country of origin.

Blink Publishing is an imprint of the Bonnier Publishing Group
www.bonnierpublishing.co.uk

CONTENTS

INTRODUCTION
THE IMPERFECT STORM

The drive from Monaco to Lausanne takes about six hours. We travelled through the night, and there wasn't a lot either of us could say to fill the time. Phil – then my fiancé, now my husband – did the driving while I sat in the front seat in the full knowledge that my entire future would hang on the next couple of days. It must have been hard for Phil to go through those hours in near silence, wondering when he would get me back from the strange mental state that had taken me over for the past few weeks. I was terrified and exhausted

We listened to the Irish folk singer Luke Kelly, one of Phil's father's favourites; he is an acquired taste, but soothing in a way. We had him on CD, as the car is too old for an iPod connection, and there are too many tunnels as you drive through the Alps for the radio to work. The Olympic Games were just over a week away, but my pre-Rio diet went out of the window; I had lost so much weight that it didn't matter whether or not I went back to my emergency motorway staple of a white Magnum ice cream or two.

Two weeks earlier, on 11 July 2016, I had been provisionally suspended by UK Anti-Doping after (UKAD) receiving three 'strikes' within the Whereabouts system that monitors an athlete's availability for random anti-drugs testing; the hearing at the Court of Arbitration (CAS) for Sport in Lausanne on 28 July would decide whether those 'strikes' stood. The first 'strike' had come when UKAD alleged I had missed a test at the World Cup round in Sweden on 20 August 2015; the second – a paperwork error rather than an actual missed test – in October that year; and the third, a missed out-of-competition test, on 9 June 2016.

The Sweden 'strike' was the strike that we decided to focus on in the hearing, as I hadn't challenged it with legal support at the time and in my heart I felt sure of discrepancies in UKAD's case due to their Doping Control Officer's (DCO) actions on that day. When he came to the team hotel at 6am and asked the hotel receptionist for my room number without any explanation, the receptionist refused to provide the number to the stranger in front of him. This was a small hotel – the only one in town – where every women's team in the World Cup was staying, and by his own admittance in court, the officer knew I was there; he just didn't try to find me. My team mechanic was at the fully branded Boels-Dolmans truck at the front of the hotel working on the bikes, and the DCO had only to go and ask him where I was, or to explain who he was or the importance of his visit, and the hotel would have obliged with my room number. He had tried to call my mobile, but it was on silent as it was 6am and I was asleep. It is not a UKAD requirement to have your mobile on at all times – and, in fact, in their rules the DCO is not allowed to phone you as it would be considered an advance warning.

I had appealed against that strike immediately to UKAD (as the rules dictate in appeals), providing what I felt was a complete explanation – and perhaps unsurprisingly since I was appealing to the organisation who had issued the strike, it was turned down. I then had the opportunity to take my appeal further, to an independent panel, but this had to be done within two weeks, and to stand any chance of success would have required me to appoint lawyers and put together a full dossier of evidence, including witnesses and statements. Aside from the cost, at that point I was in the final run-in to the world championships in Richmond, USA – I was in the form of my life, in a different time zone, part of a team working towards a team time trial title, as well the individual road race two weeks after that, and time and logistics were against me. The problem was that I didn't get a second chance for an appeal after those two weeks, unless I had received a further two strikes and had been hit with a provisional ban, which was the situation I found myself in now.

It had been an excruciating wait to learn the final date of the hearing and its location, London or Lausanne; the CAS had an immense backlog of cases as they worked through the appeals coming out of the Russian doping disaster in the run-in to the Rio Games, so we were only informed 36 hours before the hearing was to take place.

Since the third 'strike' on 9 June, and the confirmation of that strike which didn't come until two weeks later, I had begun going through all the possible life implications in my head and the enormity of the situation. There is your reputation, which you will never get back; as it is now, it's damaged, but I am not a banned athlete. I am not, never have been and never will be, a cheat, and it hurts that people might think of me as one no matter what I say or do now because of an administrative error. More personally, I was terrified about how it would affect my relationship with Phil if I was banned: I would go from being the independent person that I had become, from having a job, success and a focus, to being dependent on my husband. I hadn't realised how important my independence was to me. I need my personal focus in life, my job, my income, my contribution to our relationship. You examine everything: would I lose friends? Would we be able to pay the rent? What about my contracts – Would we stop? Would you have to pay everyone back? Would we have to move? Being banned would be monumental in the impact it would have on my life and on those around me, and all the people that had supported me as I progressed to where I was. Among it all was the fear of losing one of the things I love most in my life: cycling. Everything depended on the decision.

Most of the time, I am a daydreamer, a talker, a planner; I couldn't do any of that before the hearing because I simply had no idea what I could plan for or dream about. I would swing from one extreme to another, from thinking that a ban would be OK, that I could live with it, embracing the possibility, then falling apart at the idea of losing the identity that I have built. I'd be thinking, 'This is fine, I can deal with it, I'll go off and start a family and we will do different things', and then I would realise that I was kidding myself. That wasn't what I wanted to happen and it would be devastating after everything I have worked for and the sacrifices I, and my family, have made.

I felt that life at this time involved constant fire-fighting, one blaze breaking out after another. Put together with the situation Phil's father was in – he was suffering from terminal cancer – and trying to plan and train for the Olympic Games, I felt like my entire life was off balance and I certainly couldn't prepare properly for the biggest event of my career so far. Phil has spoken to me since about how I was at that time – so unlike myself: very emotional, very anxious, very vulnerable. One moment I would be OK, and then I would burst into tears. I was very needy – I had to be around him – very different from how I usually am. I wasn't confident at all – even months later, I haven't got that back completely. Little anxieties would lead to immense outbursts of tears. What should I pack? What should I wear so that the court would understand I am a clean athlete? I worried about every tiny and, in retrospect, irrelevant detail.

Ironically enough, as we drove north, I updated my whereabouts: overnight accommodation, Lausanne, morning one-hour testing time slot, Lausanne.

We had meetings that morning with our lawyers to go over the case; we prepared and practised our witness statements. Then we left them to work and had the rest of the day to wander aimlessly around Lausanne. Less than a week before travelling to Rio, I was sat on the edge of the lake eating a Nutella crepe, because that was the only form of calories that I could force myself to eat. This was a world away from the preparation I had planned. I counted my blessings; one small one was that I had realised how much I love cycling. Most importantly, Phil was by my side. He was my rock. This was such an intense, scary experience that I cannot begin to explain it, but what I can say is that it was so valuable – and it still is now – to have someone who went through it all with me.

* * *

The Court of Arbitration for Sport was not what I'd expected; it is housed in an ornate old bourgeois house, not a massive imposing courthouse but a Swiss mansion. Our courtroom is large, the size of a big boardroom, in between two meeting rooms where each side would take their breaks. The tables are set out in a U-shape; the three arbitrators sit in the bow of the U and the two sides face each other, with a single table opposite the arbitrators for the witnesses to give their evidence; everyone has a microphone, and there is a large television set for witnesses to give evidence via videoconference. Of the three arbitrators, you choose one, the opposing side chooses one, and there is one from within CAS itself. Before the case, your lawyers check the list of about 150 arbitrators, see what cases they have done, how they went and so on. My lawyers were concerned as they felt we had got UKAD's hard-line guy: a scary-looking, no-nonsense bloke who usually didn't show much sympathy to athletes.

The hearing was an awful experience. UKAD were sitting on the other side of the room from me – I sat next to Phil and one of my lawyers – and they were dissecting my character. Apparently I was in UKADs 'suspicious' pool because I update my whereabouts more than 200 times a year; this is obvious, because I travel a great deal, and because you have to fill in your whereabouts three months in advance, so you fill it in with your default – my home address in Monaco. Then I update that for each of the 200 days or so a year that I'm on the road racing and training, once I know my schedule. As a result, it changes a lot. The only witness I had on site was Phil; through the video link we called upon Danny Stam, my directeur sportif; Richard, the team mechanic; the hotel receptionist from where we had been staying in Sweden, and the hotel manager. UKAD called on their DCO and their head of operations

During the time that we had been waiting for the date of the hearing, my lawyers and I had been preparing to go to the court, spending hours on the phone each day going through every detail and getting witness statements and so on for each of the strikes; you have to put forward your case for each of them. After the first one, luckily enough I'd taken photos at the hotel on the morning when they came to test me. I'd had all these missed calls, and for some reason thought 'that must have been Anti-Doping', so I had the foresight to take photos of all the cars out front. Our trucks were all over the entrance, our mechanic was working there; so I had photos that were important in establishing that the DCO didn't do much looking around or try very hard to find me. He walked into the hotel, asked for my room number and when he wasn't given access to our team room list he didn't then follow the proper guidelines for locating an athlete.

For me, the hearing was very physical – my heart beating so hard it felt as if it would come out of my chest, Phil soaked in sweat and there was a knot in my stomach – but by that point I was used to feeling nauseous, ill with stress, so it wasn't too unusual. When I had to give my evidence, they asked me if I wanted to add anything – I'd written something down, a sort of a speech that expressed everything that cycling means to me:

> *I take my responsibilities as an athlete very seriously. I love sport. I am a passionate ambassador of clean sport, having the chance to compete on a level playing field is fundamental to the integrity of sport and its associated values. I have dedicated my entire adult life to trying to win Olympic gold. I represent how hard work and dedication can equal medals. I care about inspiring young athletes, in particular women, in my sport who I have fought hard for the right to equality. I have always tried to do the right thing. I am heartbroken that these events could cost me ten years of sacrifice and commitment.*

By the end of it Phil was holding back the tears. Seeing Phil becoming emotional in front of me, stumbling as he gave his evidence, was awful, because he had been so good to me, so supportive: I couldn't have got through it all without him.

The moment I dared to dream we were winning the case was when the hard-line arbitrator chosen by UKAD laughed at the evidence given by their DCO. 'This should never have come to court; you are wasting everyone's time,' he said. Then, 'That's enough, we don't need to hear any more from your witnesses', and stopped the proceedings. At that point we were told to adjourn; we came back in and they said that because it was so close to the Olympic Games they had made their decision and were telling us immediately: the Sweden strike would not stand. They gave us the option of going into the other two strikes, but we would have had to stay another day and I needed every possible second to prepare for the Games which started the following week, so I left my appeals there. CAS hearings can take up to 200 hours, so this was unprecedented; it was all over by 5pm.

Our families were on the end of the phone waiting for news – my parents were already in Rio. My dad texted my agent, Emma, asking if she had any update, and the first line of her reply came up on his screen: 'John, this is just awful.' My mum saw this, immediately assumed that the decision had gone against me, and collapsed in the middle of the road in downtown Rio. It took my dad an hour to calm her down, and they decided the best place to wait was in their hotel room even though there would be no distractions from the anguish.

I called them on FaceTime from the car and waited to see them on the screen before I smiled. I will never forget my mum's face; she grabbed my dad's neck and sobbed and sobbed. I have never seen her so vulnerable – even now it makes me emotional just thinking about it. I feel incredibly guilty that their four weeks in Brazil to celebrate my dad's retirement were ruined by the situation I was in, but I'm relieved on the other hand that they actually made the decision to go ahead with it rather than stay in Europe for me.

We drove over the Great St Bernard Pass and stopped just after the Italian border to eat a meal with the first smiles we had had on our faces for almost two months. We didn't realise that the immense relief we felt would be short-lived.

*   *   *

Chasing a gold medal at the Olympics consumes you. It is an overwhelming job; it has to be. I had no chance to think about the summer of 2016, to contemplate how my life had changed, until I had a week at home after the Rio Games. Suddenly, however, you realise you are 27 years old and a world champion; this isn't your hobby any more and you have a host of responsibilities. You are public property with all that comes with that. You can go from being a nation's hope, from people stopping your family in the street with well wishes, to seeing your photo on the front page of a national newspaper with the word 'doper' in the headline. Good and bad times are temporary, however; luckily for me, the Armitsteads give me a very firm grounding and a strong support network.

My account of the first two strikes was included in the initial draft of this book, and it was always my intention to go through the whole story in the final version to come out not long after the Olympics – including the court case at the CAS. My hope was that I would be able to give a full account of what happened during the summer of 2016 in my own time, with context and hindsight. I didn't get that opportunity; the news of my two strikes and the one that had been overturned was leaked to a newspaper in the run-in to Rio. The reaction was disproportionate, perhaps because of the timing; some of the reporting was inaccurate and the scrutiny I received did unnecessary damage to my reputation and career, as I see it.

The irony is that I want to see lifetime bans for riders who test positive. That was my position before the 'strikes' controversy and that is what it remains. There should be no second chances, because the effects of using drugs might contribute to an athlete's physical ability after a ban ends; giving them an unfair advantage. Being a professional sportsperson is a privilege, not a right. If you cheat, then that should be taken away from you, and you can do something else.

I used to be softer on this, and I am aware that there is a whole spectrum of cases: you could have a rider from a deprived background who can see doping as a way to a better economic future, for example. But my position has hardened since I have been together with Phil, who has raced as a professional since 2005. When I asked him about it, it made me really angry to learn how he had spent his early career in a period when doping was widespread, and his ambition to win was rubbed away by it. He became a domestique rather than take drugs and be a winner; I am immensely proud of him that he chose that course. I don't like competing alongside riders who have had bans and have then made comebacks to racing. It makes me very, very angry, and is unsettling because there will always be questions about their performance and their results.

There are parts of this book that have not been easy to write. I know that it will be pulled apart and dissected by people. Should I be apologetic? Should I look for sympathy? Do I write for the people who believe in me, or try to convince the ones who don't? I decided that in ten years time, when I will be living a different life, I want to look back at my book knowing that I wrote it with integrity and honesty. I want it to inspire people to be confident and enjoy cycling

I have never wanted to be famous; I have come to realise that I don't have any control over whether people I don't know like me or not. I am a cyclist first and foremost, not a celebrity, so I want to tell you my story from the perspective of a normal girl from Otley who skipped a maths lesson and went on to win a world championship. Writing a book that I can stand proudly behind is the most important thing for me and the people I care about. As far as I'm concerned, everything begins with them: my family and my friends.

CHAPTER 1

HOME

The photographs stuck on the wall of our apartment in Monaco are a reminder of life outside the cycling bubble, of the people who really matter to me, the times and places when I've been happiest. Monaco isn't my true home: I live here because cycling has brought me here and because it's one of the best places to be when you earn a living from bike racing, but when my time in the sport is over I will move out again.

At the top, there's a picture of my grandma and granddad, Ray and Marjorie – my mum's parents – in the woods, giving each other a hug. They usually both wear the same rain jacket because Grandma is always in charge of what Granddad wears, which I still find funny. They both live in Otley, which is where I was brought up – my grandmother is the lady you will see at races in a yellow T-shirt with 'I'm Lizzie Armitstead's grandma' on it.

Although they have both turned 80 they are still very active. They go on cruises around the world, where you are only allowed to have hand luggage, so they take Brompton folding bikes that fit into the bags; that way, Grandma can roll up her dresses and put them in with her bike and they can go exploring when the boat docks somewhere new. So when they land, they come down the gangplank, turn right or turn left, ride on their Brompton bikes for half a day, and then they come back to the boat.

Grandma worked until she was 65 – she was a very talented

textiles teacher – whereas Granddad was made redundant in his fifties and became a househusband; he still does all the cleaning and cooking, which I suppose is quite unusual for that generation. When I was a youngster, Granddad would pick me up from school on a Tuesday and would look after me while Grandma was still at work. But he was also the town mayor in Otley. That's probably where I first saw gender equality in practice; it didn't ever really occur to me that you could be put into a box because you are a woman or a man. My grandparents are just great people, very, very loving and generous; if I ever needed anything I could talk to them and they would help me out.

Back on my apartment wall, next to the picture of my grandparents, is a picture of my mum and dad, Carol and John, when they were younger, giving each other a hug on their Sunday walk. I just love that photo because they both look perfectly happy. They are great role models for me; they are still very much in love after thirty years of marriage and they never let anything affect their relationship. That meant as kids, my brother and sister and me had to learn to be independent; I like that. If Mum and Dad had booked a romantic weekend in the Lake District, then we would be told, 'Take care of yourselves, kids, there's stuff in the freezer.' That would be the answer – it worked because we are spread in age over six years – and that's something I admire. They've both worked hard, and I feel very privileged to have been brought up the way I have.

Dad has been an accountant since he left school but he has never really enjoyed his job; it doesn't suit him being confined to an office every day. Perhaps that's why whenever we had spare time as a family, so much of it was spent outside. Our family is religious on both sides, but despite this my dad is an unbudging atheist. As a family we went to church until I was around 12 or 13; Dad would rarely come, preferring to go for a solitary bike ride in the Dales instead. I can't help looking forward to seeing what adventures he will share with my mum in retirement, which will give him the freedom he has always craved.

Next comes a picture of me and my sister Kate when

she came to visit me while I was living in Belgium. Kate's probably my best friend: at 33 she is six years older than me, and she has two children, Amelia and Austin. We're really close.

That night in Belgium, we went out to have an ice cream; I can tell from my face how happy I am at seeing her again, because I have missed her so much. It was back before she had children, so she was a little bit drunk and happy. Kate is not into competitive sport, although she is pretty active, but that means the two of us are not in competition with each other at all. She works as a social re-development officer in Bradford, so she tackles gender issues, race issues, all sorts of things, and loves it. She inspires me to be confident: her political beliefs, particularly on equality, are very important to her. She is very maternal too – she always looked after me in the school holidays and has guided me through some difficult periods in my life – although I suppose that relationship shifted a bit when she had Amelia, her oldest.

Then there is Nick, my brother, the middle child – I am the youngest – who is 30, three years older than me and works as a plumber. The picture on my wall shows him with a big pint in his hand and a big smile on his face. He doesn't have his picture taken very often, but I caught him off guard one time when he came to pick me up from the airport and we went to get a pint in the local pub before we went home. Nick struggled with confidence as a kid; I was always the same height as him and even though he was three years older than me he was a skinny lad, so I am quite protective of him. He is quite shy, very similar to my dad. He always used to hate road racing. When I really started getting into bike racing, he was a downhill mountain biker and called us 'roadies' – the off-roaders always thought that 'roadies' wore Lycra that is too tight and the shaved legs were weird. That all turned on its head when he came to watch the criterium in the centre of Otley; I was riding in it that year – in the men's race, as per usual – and that sparked his interest. For some reason, he thought, 'I could be good at this' and he took up road cycling. It really helped him with his confidence, and now when I go home I have someone to train with. He would be my 'phone a friend' on

Who Wants to be a Millionaire? – he is full of useless but riveting facts.

Among the photographs of my family I've scattered a few of people who are close to me and have supported me over the years. Next to Nick is one of me and my agent Emma Wade at bespoke M. It was the first picture I had taken after I won the silver medal in London; in fact it was my first personal picture with my actual medal. Emma is in my 'team', one of the small group of people who are close to me and who have helped me with my career over the years. I am very lucky that I started out with her in 2009; she has been my agent ever since and I can't imagine changing to another. Emma manages all aspects of my career and

sometimes that spills over into my personal life too; without her I wouldn't have managed to maintain the balance I have now. Having another woman alongside me in recent years has been invaluable.

Then there is a picture of Az, a good friend who goes back to year seven in high school: he has a big bratwurst in his hand at the German Christmas Market in Leeds in December 2012. He suffers from lupus, which is an auto-immune disease; there is no cure, you go through episodes that can range in severity, but if you are unlucky it can kill you, so he

is on auto-immune depressants. He had just recovered from his most severe episode and that's a nice memory because he looked so healthy again, back to being the life and soul of the party and offering out his usual bear hugs.

There is a snap of me and Westy – Phil West, my first coach, the guy who got me into cycling in the first place – on the wall as well; that was one I had to have, again because

it's a moment when he was really happy. It was taken at a charity race, which we rode together, when he had shed loads of weight after putting on a fair bit once he stopped racing himself. He dropped about 30 kilos, so for me to be able to race with him again after he lost all that was lovely. I felt proud of him in the way that he had been proud of me as a racer.

I also have a picture up there of Phil, my husband, in his Irish national cycling team gear. I'm fond of that one because he is wearing a Catlike helmet – white with lots of round holes, any cycling fan should remember them – which is the type we both wore when we rode for the Cervélo team in 2010. That was several years before we got together, but it was a time when we were teammates, and I like being reminded of that. You can underestimate what it feels like to represent your country or take it for granted. But it is something to admire, so this picture is a reminder of that as well. I feel very proud of Phil when I look at that picture; I am not supposed to have pictures of him cycling up in the house, but I snuck that one up because I don't want him to overlook what he has achieved.

Then there is Amelia, my niece at two years old, placed on the wall a little bit along from her mum Kate. This was different: I just remember holding her in my arms as a newborn and having an overwhelming sense of love for her, which was something I didn't expect. My love for my family is like no other and the instant she was born, the number

of people I loved that way grew by one. As a baby she was effectively a stranger but I instantly felt a bond with her, and that was really special. Next to it I have another one of Phil, in Key West, on our holiday in Miami in 2014. That was the first holiday we went on together. In that moment I remember registering that I was immensely happy, feeling completely content.

I've got a similar feeling about a photo of me at my friends' Paul and Laura Di Resta's wedding in Florence in 2014. I'm standing with Pippa, my closest friend in Monaco, and Jen, another friend and neighbour, on the Ponte Vecchio; all the guests are about to get on three coaches to go up to the castle where Paul and Laura were married. This day was also special because I got around a clash with the cycling calendar

to get there. The wedding was between the penultimate World Cup round at Vårgårda in Sweden and the last one, the GP Plouay, and I had been debating whether I could go. I managed to win overall with a round to spare after Sweden, so I was able to make it to the wedding and have a blast – it was a really good night, one where I managed to coax myself into unwinding. The smile on my face is so genuine; I had won the Commonwealth Games a few weeks before adding the World Cup, and it was one of the rare occasions when I found myself completely switched off from cycling. I was absorbed in Paul and Laura's day, completely content again.

And there is a picture of Finlay, Westy's little boy, who was effectively my little brother for a short while. When I

lived with Westy and his family, I was riding full-time on the Great Britain team and Finlay was always a little mate to come home to after a rubbish track session. He's six now, so back then he was a little buddy to lift my spirits. Another one is a picture of me and Beth, who is my oldest friend; we are incredibly similar and I can tell from a single look between the two of us that we are thinking the same thing. We were sat next to each other in year three; our class was too big for the classroom, so we were almost in the corridor and we got up to a fair bit of mischief. We have been good

friends ever since; now, she is doing a training contract at a solicitor's in Leeds.

Beth is also in the photo of my 21st birthday, together with Az and three other friends that I am still incredibly close to now: Sam, with whom I had a brief romance in year eight before we decided we were better off as friends; Dom, who is the real lad among the group, constantly finding some funny tale to cheer us up, and Ben, who is a geography teacher now, something I can't get my head around. The six of us are a dysfunctional, close-knit group, but somehow we are perfectly matched, and with them, I feel completely myself.

Finally, there is a photo of Phil and his family. Phil wasn't

keen on having photos on the wall, so I snuck one up among all the others. I'm working on his sentimental side.

* * *

My mum and dad met at church when they were 11 and have been together since they were 16. I'm the third child, born in Leeds, just like my brother and sister were. We've all been brought up to be independent – not independent of each other, but able to look after ourselves. Mum and Dad's relationship is very important to them, so rather than their lives being centred around us, we have always fitted around the things they do, as well as our own activities. It feels quite a contrast to the way many children are brought up these days.

My mum's family lived in Beeston, near Leeds and then moved to Otley, which was where my mum grew up. My dad was born in Garstang, which is in Lancashire, and then moved to Otley with his family. He's one of five children – there were four girls and my dad. When he was about 11, not long after moving to Otley, he joined the church and met my mum and pursued her for four years.

As kids, we would go to church every Sunday morning, but we would go with Mum. My dad would go off on a bike ride; he never came to church although he helped to run the church youth group on Friday night. He understood the importance of the church and the community and he likes the people there and so on, but he's an atheist and he's not going to be persuaded to be otherwise. His weekends were very important to him and so were his evenings.

We were always busy. My mum ran Guides and took my sister along too. Me and Nick went to Scouts when the Guides disbanded later on. Mum and Dad would also go to running club every Tuesday and Thursday, and Dad would take me to my running club on a Wednesday night. There would be a race most weekends as well. We didn't stop there: I'd go swimming on Tuesday night – I'd walk to that as well – and Dad would run the youth club on a Friday.

During the week there would be walks, bike rides, family visits and so on.

As a child, I assumed that's what everyone did: fill your evenings with activities rather than just sit at home. My childhood was spent outside as much as possible – in fact, we were made to get out of the house, with a walk every Sunday, for example, which I just hated. We would either drive somewhere in the car for about 20 minutes or set out on a walk from the house, but every Sunday there would have to be some kind of activity.

My mum is the total opposite of my dad. She retrained after having children and became a teacher. Now she works in a college teaching teenagers, and she seems to teach everything. She started off in IT, which we all find hilarious because if the computer is broken, Mum just turns it off and on again. She is what I would call 'a blagger', my mum, constantly bluffing her way around things, and with a gift for getting the most out of things. She loves sport for different reasons to my dad: she enjoys the social aspect and is great at encouraging other people. She is an organiser: our school holidays were planned out and packed with activities. If you need something doing, she is the person to ask.

My dad is the straightest man you could come across. I remember getting a free train trip when I was a kid because I didn't see the guard to buy a ticket. When Mum picked me up, her reaction was, 'Well done, but don't tell your dad!' He wouldn't mind now, but back then I never did tell him.

Later, when I used to bunk off school to go on bike rides, Mum used to say, 'Lizzie, if you can teach yourself better than the teacher can, and as long as you catch up, I have no problem with you skiving, just don't tell your dad.' Whereas my dad would never have seen it like that.

Dad would go out on his bike on Sunday mornings, but that had nothing to do with me eventually becoming a cyclist. He's never been a member of a cycling club or anything of that kind; he's never raced, he just enjoys his own company. He's very much his own man: he's a thinker and he likes to go off and do stuff. He still does. For example, he and my mum are both members of the Otley running club and he has completed marathons like the Bob Graham run – a challenge in the Lake District, which lasts 72 miles and ascends 42 peaks in 24 hours. He's not competitive with other people, but he takes on longer or tougher challenges than most.

Our house is on the outskirts of Otley, which is a small town on the edge of Leeds. It has lots of churches, charity shops, pubs and fish-and-chip shops. The river Wharfe runs through the middle and as a six-year-old I became the youngest girl to compete in the river Wharfe race, which is essentially a 1km scurry in muddy water. The Chevin is the hill that sits to the south, with Leeds–Bradford airport on top. Our house is on the main road towards Harrogate, so if I turn right I can go on a four-hour ride without seeing a traffic light; if you go west up the valley you can do beautiful hilly rides towards Kettlewell and Grassington. If you head east, you get to the flatter roads towards Wetherby and York.

We all went to the Whartons Primary school, up a cul-de-sac on the edge of Otley, and I always walked there with my brother and sister, which took about ten minutes. It wasn't large – about 200 pupils – but there was a huge playing field. For some reason, Beth and I always ended up organising things together – we ran around the school field cross-legged in wellies filled with baked beans for Children in Need, and organised a bring-and-buy sale for *Blue Peter*. We played clarinet together for a while, too; I wanted to be good at something other than sport, but I wasn't great at it. Beth was even worse because her fingers were too small to get over the holes. We laughed a lot about that.

Mum stayed at home for us working different jobs and irregular shifts until we had all started school, then she returned to full-time work. That's when we were picked up every Tuesday by Granddad: I remember that because I used to be so embarrassed by him: he would always ride his bike to school and he would turn up in pink, turquoise, see-through Lycra, and he wouldn't be shy about talking to people. After all, he was the mayor of Otley. But he was a fantastic granddad; we used to go back to his house and play dominoes every Tuesday while we waited for my mum to finish work and pick me up.

I was very much given the freedom to do the things I wanted as a kid, but whenever I joined a club or began an activity, I would *always* have to pay my subs at the start of that term and have to commit to it. It was never a case of 'If you change your mind, you don't have to go any more'. If I was going somewhere to do something, I had to follow it through.

Looking back on my childhood, I now appreciate the way that Mum and Dad brought us up. We weren't spoilt; you'd hold out until your birthday to get something you always wanted, it wasn't just given to you. I suppose I resented that a little, because my friends were going swimming or going to McDonald's, and those things were huge treats in our house. For example, Coca-Cola was not a given in our house – it was a Christmas thing – whereas I would go to a friend's house and they would have it. At the time, it was frustrating not having the things my school friends had, but I would always try to come up with a solution. I was constantly coming up with payment plans – such as figuring out how many times I would have to wash the car to get this or that. That probably came from my mum.

We were not given luxuries on demand but I have to say we were spoilt for holidays; in fact, time away together was a priority. We were perfectly well off, I would say, but Mum would shop in Netto and we would go on three holidays a year. We'd go skiing every year, then camping in France for three weeks in the summer, and we'd cap the year off with a holiday in October as well. Most of our holidays were in France or Switzerland and, looking back, the trips to the mountains of Switzerland stood out the most, but I think at the time I was probably asking my parents, 'Why are we in these stupid boring campsites in the middle of nowhere?'

I remember one story in particular. We hiked up from Zermatt to the Matterhorn in Switzerland, my brother, my dad, my mum and me (my sister was too old by this point to come on holiday with us). We were starving by the time we got to the top – we were so hungry – and me and my brother had to share a portion of chips and a Coke because it was so expensive. Mum got the cable car home, and we had to walk back down the hill. It was an incredible experience, but I probably moaned all the way down.

I did enjoy primary school. The Whartons was a small community school where everyone knew everyone. I was always close to the top, or average, never the best but pretty good. Moving to high school took a bit more getting used to. I attended Prince Henry's, which was the only big school in Otley. You lose your primary school friends when you join the seniors, and my elder sister had left the year before I arrived, so it was just me and my brother there, and when we were that age Nick and I hated each other, so he wasn't a great deal of help.

High school felt like a means to an end, but every playtime was filled with netball or hockey, and in the sports teams I found my place a little bit. I did just about every sport going – swimming, hockey, netball, cross-country, football. I was in pretty much every team and if the team in the year above us were missing a hockey player, for example, I would play for them as well. I was physically fit enough to be fairly good at everything because of my running and swimming, but I was short on skill. In football I was the worst goalkeeper ever – we lost two tournaments because I kept coming out of my area and giving away penalties. Beth, on the other hand, ended up playing for Bradford City until she was 16. She never did pursue the clarinet.

The reason it took me a while to find exactly who my friends were at Prince Henry's was that phenomenon at school where the popular kids were the sporty kids. I didn't really click with the popular group, so I was a bit in between: my friends wouldn't be coming to netball practice, but I didn't really want to hang around with the netball team when we weren't playing.

To begin with, I was quite inspired by the idea of becoming a serious runner. I used to go running every Tuesday and Thursday with the local running club Skyrac, and I definitely ran because I knew my parents liked it. I was pretty competitive. There was a school cross-country for the local schools in year six and my granddad – who is an armchair sportsman and thinks that he knows everything about everything – ran across to each corner of the playing field to tell me to run at nine miles an hour because that's what he had calculated I needed to do to win the race.

I did win the race, but looking back we had an unusual way of approaching it. The other kids who were at that level had parents there with water bottles, and wore spikes and those running knickers; I was wearing some of my sister's old shorts, my school T-shirt and trainers. And I had my granddad there. *And* the night before I had been up late and dancing: it was my parents' fortieth birthday, after all, so we all got together to celebrate. I just didn't take the running that seriously.

But perhaps I should have done, because once I was in year six – the last year of primary school, as a 10- or 11-year-old – I was selected to represent Leeds in an international for twin cities, to run the 800m and 1500m. My mum dropped me off at the bus station in Leeds for the 30-hour trip to Dortmund, which was twinned with Leeds; I had to do the journey with about 20 other kids, parents and staff from the City of Leeds Athletic Club. I used to get crippling nerves when I was running – absolutely awful – and on the bus, I was petrified. I remember crying, and pretending I had something in my eye. Once we were there, I loved it; it was an amazing experience. I was clearly pretty good at running, but I had started puberty early, and once all the other girls caught up I no longer had the edge. I didn't have a runner's body any more, so I lost interest.

I didn't realise until recently that I have inherited my dad's need for space, in all senses of the word. I love being outside. Our upbringing was centred on embracing outdoor activities and, being from Yorkshire, the cheaper the better (free if possible). The countryside is so accessible from where we lived that we didn't need to get in a car to go for a walk in the fields. I love seeing wide-open spaces, which is part of being on the bike. Views are crucial to me – later, when I went to live in Manchester and trained daily on the velodrome there, my brain felt starved of good views.

Being an athlete is a transitory matter: your teammates change each year; you move around constantly from place to place rarely seeing much outside the race bubble; careers don't last long. Given the strength of the connection I feel to those who are close to me, and to the place where I was brought up, it's not surprising that in my cycling career I've looked for stability by giving my loyalty to a small group of people in whom I have absolute trust. I figure out whom I want to stick with, and I stick with them.

My family life is woven into the fabric of Otley – my granddad being the mayor, my parents running youth clubs and Guides, my dad being the accountant for the Otley Churches' Christian Aid collection, in spite of being an atheist. Having three children from one family go through the school system makes your world smaller; even now, having a brother who is a plumber there means getting a quote from a local tradesman is a bit easier as well. My roots are in Otley and there is a sense of permanence about Yorkshire that contrasts with the travelling circus of international sport. Otley is a community. I am part of that, and that is something I didn't realise was unusual until I left.

CHAPTER 2

THE SECRET
SOCIETY

There are moments that take your life in a certain direction. This was one of them, and it came just before my 15th birthday.

It was during a maths lesson when one of the PE teachers – either Miss Grant or Miss Temple – knocked on the door. 'Lizzie, Shernaz' – Shernaz was one of my friends – 'come with me, come and have a go at this.' I remember it being a fine sunny day, just before the summer holidays in 2003. All the kids who were any good at sport had been told to gather on the school playing field to perform in a series of sports tests. Shernaz and I weren't entirely sure what we were letting ourselves in for, but as we gathered on the field we noticed a few guys who I now know were from the British

Cycling Talent Team – including Phil West, Jonny Clay and Claire Rushworth – stood next to some cones, readying the sports field for a series of timed sprints and endurance races.

I was just pootling around, chatting to the other girls on the field, when I heard a familiar-sounding voice. 'Come on, Lizzie... bet you can't beat me!'

It was Richard Robinson – or 'Little Richard' – a cheeky ginger-haired chap who had been my first boyfriend back in primary school. He stood at the first cone, waiting for me to pick up a bike and race him along the field.

It was a challenge I couldn't resist: I picked up a bike and raced him across the stretch of the cones set up for the test, keeping up with Richard before eventually powering past him. At the time I had just planned on riding around and perhaps even missing my maths lesson; little did I know, as I beat Richard across the finish line, that Phil West and his team were watching the riders very closely.

'Talent Team' was a pretty basic screening system that British Cycling had brought in after the Sydney Olympics in 2000 to try and identify new talent. Recent graduates from the scheme included Olympic medallists such as Jo Rowsell, Dani King, Ed Clancy and Jason Kenny – all of whom began there. It was run on a regional basis by coaches who travelled out into schools that wanted to join up, and had several stages that took you further and further into the British Cycling system.

Beating Richard seemed to indicate that I had some sort

of talent. Phil West took my name down, and I probably exaggerated how good I was when I got home. Dad thought I was being ridiculous, but then a letter came during the long summer holidays: I had got through to the next trial.

The second stage was in a school hall in Bradford, which was a 45-minute journey by car – a fair way to go just to perform a cycling assessment. By now it was getting into winter, so I went with my mum after she finished work, and she also dragged my brother along for the ride. I'm not sure how seriously my mum viewed it, because neither of us knew a great deal about what we were doing. And then, when I walked into the school hall, I saw the turbo trainers and power cranks and thought, 'I'm going to be rubbish at this.' What made it worse was that all the other parents were there with their kids, all with their water bottles, whereas I was so unprepared that I was still wearing my hockey skirt.

My mum and brother both sat there while I did the test on the turbo trainer, and again I came away thinking, 'I have no chance; I must have been rubbish.' But it must have gone well, too, as I was then invited to the third step – an induction camp in Horsforth, just up the hill from Otley.

Phil West ran the camp, where we did more tests, and were forced to drink a litre of milk and a banana – I imagine now that it was some kind of primitive protein drink – and I remember thinking, 'This is horrible.' They also weighed us, recorded our height, gave us a load of kit – clothing, helmets, shoes, which was the cool bit – and lots of Persil washing powder vouchers; the whole talent system was sponsored by them, right up to the under-23 teams.

At the end of the camp there was a rider–parent conference to explain to us what we were getting into. My mum put her hand up and asked, 'About this five hundred pounds of Lottery funding – how will you know if they don't spend it on cycling things?' It was a perfectly reasonable question, but it emphasised how little she and I knew about the sport: a lot of the other kids were already riding with cycling clubs, they and their parents were well informed, they understood the language of the sport, and they were all immensely enthusiastic about bike racing because they wanted their child to be the next Nicole Cooke or Chris Hoy. We were just blagging our way through, with an attitude of 'It sounds all right, let's show up and see what happens.' I felt like a total fraud.

Despite the encouraging start at the training camp it took a while for the cycling bug to bite. That winter I went to watch a World Cup in Manchester with Anna Blyth, who was to ride for several years with British Cycling, eventually turning into a world-class sprinter. Anna was only six months older than me, but she was a year ahead at school and so had joined up 12 months before me; we had to share a room at one of the camps, where all the younger girls were placed in a room with an older rider. I really looked up to her: she was a long way ahead of me, and had already won medals at the national championships. She lived just ten minutes from

Otley and reminded me of Beth: straight-talking, sarcastic and funny.

Anna and I got the bus from Leeds to the event in Manchester but we missed the last one home and Anna's dad had to come and get us. We got into trouble for that, but I remember thinking, 'Aaahh, I get it. That's it. I want to be good at this.' I liked the sleekness and the speed of track cycling. I felt like such an amateur putting on these big overshoes to go out on the road in the winter, and this big uncomfortable helmet. It never felt fast training in Yorkshire in the winter; I never got a sense of excitement from it, but being in the velodrome where there was a full audience, seeing the skinsuits and disc wheels, I finally caught sight of the shiny part of cycling. I can't recall any particular events I liked – I still didn't know enough about what I was seeing – but I remember seeing Vicky Pendleton and Chris Hoy. They were the first cyclists I thought were cool. I certainly didn't think that riding around Otley. There were no cool cyclists there.

In fact, getting into cycling in Otley – like in most parts of Britain in those days – was like joining a secret society. I used to spot a few cyclists on the road outside my house when I was a kid: they would speed past while I was playing with my own bike, which was actually my brother's old mountain bike. I was always given hand-me-down bikes until about the age of 12, after which I didn't own a bike or play with one outside my house. Looking back, I suspect it was because you

31

usually get a bike for Christmas, and I didn't want to waste my Christmas present on a bike. That all changed, of course, when I was spotted by Phil West racing Little Richard on the school fields. But I had no knowledge of bike racing or its history: I hadn't heard of Chris Boardman, Nicole Cooke or any of the major British figures of recent years. Until the Talent Team gave me a bike, I didn't own one.

I tried to go out on rides with the locals, but you had to find out who they were and where they met by word of mouth, just by asking around. It's hugely improved now, but back then there was no Facebook or Twitter; it was 'meet at the third lamp post at five to six on a Tuesday'. I never did manage to find out who the local cyclists were; I was just too nervous, I didn't know anybody there and they were all older blokes, so I just didn't bother. Later, however, I came across the local chain gang on a Tuesday and Thursday and that was fantastic, if not brutal, training. I still get involved with that when I go home now.

Not being part of a club, I joined British Cycling as a private member, but because you needed a team, I signed up with Chevin Cycles, the local bike shop. I tried to get kit from them but they didn't stock anything small enough; all I could find was a pair of shorts that cost £70 – which was a bit extravagant from my mum's point of view. And that made it all the more frustrating when I ripped the shorts in a heavy crash at my first race.

The Future Stars series which took place at the Revolution

meetings in the Manchester velodrome are now a fixture in British cycling, but back then they were just beginning. The Revolutions – held just at Manchester at first, but now at London, Derby and Glasgow too – had started out as a way of showing stars like Chris Hoy, Vicky Pendleton and Bradley Wiggins to the public. Future Stars was slotted into the meetings to give up-and-coming under-16s experience of racing in a championship environment: sell-out crowds, a lot of stars hanging around in the pits, real atmosphere. The series is a huge thing now, because of the exposure you can get as a youngster. I still ride the senior Revolution meetings occasionally; they had me back for an omnium against Marianne Vos after the 2012 Olympics.

Back then my parents didn't really understand the scale of the event. They didn't know that the Revolutions meant 6,000 people cramming the velodrome. With that in mind they were happy for me to grab a lift to the velodrome with Anna. But there were kids there who had brought both parents along as their helpers; they had rollers to warm up on, and water bottles. Just as when I ran regional races, I still didn't have any of that stuff. I was so nervous. I was sat there in the corner, absolutely bricking it.

The Revolutions felt like part of the aforesaid secret society: I didn't understand any of it. Take the Welsh: national funding meant they had what was almost a professional set-up, so the Welsh girls who rode on the Newport track all had skinsuits. I didn't even know what a skinsuit was; I had shorts and a jersey. They all had disc wheels, they had team tactics and I was just hanging on for dear life, thinking, 'Right, what am I doing here?' They all wore sunglasses and I remember thinking, 'Why wear sunglasses indoors?'

I had something on my side though: I was part of the North-West Talent Team and all our training camps used to be on the track in Manchester, which meant Phil West – or Westy as we were now calling him – had had us doing all sorts of exercises there. For example, even as a 15-year-old I had been doing Madison – the relay with two riders where one rests, one races and you 'throw' your partner into the action – which meant I had a high skill level compared to most of the other riders, who didn't get to train on an indoor velodrome as often. The disparity in skill levels probably contributed to a huge crash, which I still have splinters from – blue splinters that haven't worked their way out – and I ripped my new shorts. But the worst thing about it was that there was a lad from Otley who had been selected as well; his parents were massively into it, so he had everything, all the kit, and he had lent me his Chevin Cycles jersey to race in. That got ruined as well.

That spring, I crashed in my first circuit race as well, which was a handicap on the roads around the police headquarters in Middlesbrough – it was an event that the Talent Team took us to, so I can't say I rode it out of choice. I started in the group with the under-12 boys and as we were lapped, another girl – Annie Simpson, who is still racing at a good level – came past me and we locked handlebars as we came into the finish together.

In 2004, I discovered the Otley town centre criterium, which takes place every July, but I had never been aware of this event that took place right on my doorstep, which shows my lack of knowledge back then. The Otley 'crit' in 2004 was a landmark; the first race I entered for myself using an official – and slightly impenetrable – British Cycling entry form.

The Otley crit is an institution in Yorkshire cycling that draws people out to watch on one night a year. There was no women's race at Otley until 2014, so for years I would ride the men's race, open to second, third and fourth categories, which was definitely the hard option. When they brought in the women's race, I rode both that and the men's.

* * *

My family's lack of cycling knowledge served me well in the long run. I would go further: it has probably been fundamental in my success. There were girls around me whose parents were deeply involved in the sport and who were regularly driving them here, there and everywhere, but since my parents did not feel cycling was the be-all and end-all, I was still catching the train with my bike to training camps because I genuinely wanted to go. Also, because I didn't have pushy parents, I enjoyed a teenage life as well. My mum and dad weren't irresponsible, but at 16 I managed to get away with more life experiences than I probably should have at that age. Other girls who had been racing all their lives were discovering drinking and partying just at the time I was coming across cycling. I didn't have the fear of missing out like them; going clubbing was good fun, I love to dance, but indulging in it like most teenagers want to just wasn't my thing.

I had to acquire a lot of my cycling knowledge off my own back, but there were key moments when my parents did help me out. They would step in when it really mattered: the first time I got my own bike, for example. I have never actually bought my own bike – if I'd had to, I might not be where I am now. Each of us were given a bike by the Talent Team from Trek – it was a cyclo-cross bike which you could use on the road if you wanted – and there was a track bike as well. When I turned junior in 2005, Westy put me in touch with the Raleigh women's team – Jenny Middlehurst was also a member – so I was given a Raleigh bike; my dad drove me to Norfolk to get it. That's a long way from Leeds, with a lot of speed cameras on the way. Additionally, when I first started training and had no one to go with; Dad would come out with me in the dark after work, because he knew I was too nervous to go on my own.

The Lottery funding that my mum had asked about at the meeting came in handy straight away when I ripped the Otley Chevin kit I'd borrowed and had to replace. Five hundred pounds felt massive, and there was no asking for receipts or any follow-up. The next item I bought was a turbo trainer, because I had got the idea that I needed to improve, and I couldn't always go out on my bike after dark, so having some way of training indoors was the solution. I decided to write my own training programme: it consisted of taking my stereo into the garage, where I would ride 'song on, song off' for an hour. I'd listen to terrible music – R&B, love songs, Westlife, Beyoncé, Destiny's Child, stuff like that. I didn't have particularly good taste but for interval training this had advantages: the intervals aren't the same length and it's easier to time them by listening to something than by constantly looking at a stopwatch.

I would kill myself like that every day, completely wear myself out, but ironically that was because I didn't take cycling all that seriously at first. I didn't want to give up on the other things I was doing, but I just didn't have the time in the week to squeeze it all in. I was still doing all of my PE as well, plus hockey matches and everything else. At weekends, I played hockey, only missing a match when I had a race with the Talent Team. There were extra-curricular activities every lunchtime, every day after school and Saturdays on top. When I look back now I wonder how on earth I did it all.

Part of the reason why I got into this state of exhaustion was that I did not yet have a strong relationship with Westy. I had been going on the training camps but otherwise I was left to my own devices. I didn't show that much interest, and because Phil only had a certain amount of time, he could only afford to devote most of his attention to the people who were taking an obvious interest; as a result, he didn't really monitor me. Eventually, my PE teacher noticed how exhausted I was. She called the Talent Team, and the upshot was that Phil came round to my house to investigate. He was clearly a bit surprised: 'Oh, you do like cycling then!'

Something else happened that winter to fire my interest. When we were on holiday in Cuba, I read a book someone had lent me: *It's Not About the Bike* by Lance Armstrong. The precise date when I read it will always stick in my mind, because it was the time of the Boxing Day tsunami. Armstrong is obviously *persona non grata* now, but back then his book inspired me. It wasn't the comeback from cancer that struck a chord: at this stage in my life, fortunately, I had never been affected by the disease, and I had yet to meet anyone who had had it, so that wasn't something that resonated with me. What struck me was that, like me, Armstrong didn't come from a cycling family. He had started off in triathlon – I had done a few of those myself – and it was the kind of book that explained cycling for a layman, the French culture and so on. It drew you into road cycling.

Once Westy felt I might have potential and commitment, he started to coach me more specifically – giving me the basics of a training plan, discussing how to balance my cycling with the other things I was doing in my life. After a little bit of talking me up, he managed to get me into the next level of British Cycling's youth development system in spring 2005, the newly formed Olympic Development Programme. I felt I was there to make up the numbers; I wasn't really shining, simply doing my own thing. But all the work we had been doing up to then had been on the track, and when finally went for a road ride in the Cheshire lanes, around Jodrell Bank, I was the strongest. I remember thinking 'cool', although ironically I came to hate that circuit later on because I ended up spending too many hours around there.

There was also a Madison session, where I was the best as well, and that helped me into the selection process for the European under-23 and junior championships that June. It came down to me, Kim Blythe, Anna Blyth, Jo Tindley – who raced for VC Londres and is still racing for Team WNT – and Jenny Middlehurst, who was from Barnsley and had been racing since she was very young. In the end, after some track testing in Newport, they took me and Jo.

* * *

Westy was to be my main guide through the world of cycling, but my cycling education took another turn in July 2005, when I started going out with Kim's brother, Adam, who was also on the Talent Team. The Blythes are from Sheffield, an hour from Otley, a train journey I have done too many times. They were a full-on complete bike-racing family, cycling mad, with all the equipment you can possibly imagine. Kim and Adam would arrive in the car park to race and train with the Talent Team with shiny suitcases, shiny shoes, shiny everything, whereas I was the amateur with no idea and all the rubbish kit. I remember as a young girl being attracted to that – and through them, and through Adam's ambitions, I decided to become a professional cyclist. With them, I learnt about cycling as a whole.

My racing experience was still very limited. I was a first-year junior; I had only ridden in the UK – criteriums and the odd road race – and I'd never done an international of any kind. Junior women didn't have their own race calendar in the UK – 2016 was the first year they even had their own national race series – so whenever we raced we were thrown straight in with the senior women, which meant anybody right up to Nicole Cooke.

The biggest event I'd ridden was that April's Cheshire Classic, a well-established race with what felt like a massive climb to the finish. I was still riding my cyclo-cross bike. It was intimidating: I had to take off my saddlebag, lose the light brackets from the bike, and bring food with me. In spite of all that, I came in fifth, beating the other girls I considered were good: Anna, Kim and Jenny. That year, it was won by Rachel Heal, who went on to ride for Great Britain, and is now working as a directeur sportif at the United Healthcare team, managing both men and women. In second place was Nikki Harris (now Brammeier), who is now my teammate at Boels-Dolmans and was at my side in the Rio Olympics; she too was at the start of her career.

* * *

The 2005 European under-23 and junior championships was probably the best trip I've ever been on with Great Britain. It was on the outdoor track in Fiorenzuola, Italy, held in baking heat. As a team we were young and inexperienced and, because we didn't know what we were doing, there was no pressure on our shoulders. Sharing a room with Anna was good fun, the sun was shining, I'd got my new GB kit to wear, and I thought it was amazing.

The points race didn't go well, however, and in the scratch I was given the job of leading Anna out for the sprint. I didn't mind working for her, because I knew she was better than me, but it meant that I finished last. I had never expected that I might win a medal, and I was delighted that she had come second, but in my mind that settled it for the next target: the junior world championships in mid-August. I wouldn't be going to the Worlds, because, in my eyes, I had been rubbish. It wasn't a disaster though: I'd be going on holiday with Mum and Dad instead.

Shane Sutton was running the team at this one. This was the first time I had come across him; the Australian was in his early days at British Cycling, and I was scared of him. Watching him in action, you felt that he was the big boss: he needed to be respected. Everyone was quiet around him. He definitely had that kind of aura: he was straight talking and, at the age of 16, I was intimidated. It came into focus when, in typical British Cycling style, we had a meeting at the team hotel at the end of the championships where everyone would be told who was going to the Worlds, and who wasn't. They sat me down, and Sutton pulled no punches. 'Because you finished last in the scratch race, you are going to the Worlds.' It was an eye-opener; one of the first times I understood about teamwork in cycling.

Great Britain cycling was a long way from where it is now. We were all given one T-shirt each with Great Britain cycling team printed on it. At the Europeans, we didn't have disc wheels; those came when we went to the Junior Worlds, which they took more seriously. I took it more seriously, too: I had a two-and-a-half-week gap between races, and when my training programme came from Westy, he had put a three-hour ride in. 'Oh God,' I thought, that's a long way.'

Something else changed: I hadn't wanted to ride my bike to school, and had been reticent about letting on about what I was doing on my bike. I didn't like the idea of being seen in my Lycra, but since I now had my GB kit from the Europeans to train in every day, I didn't mind if my friends saw me on my bike. All of a sudden, I wasn't embarrassed about being a cyclist.

At the Junior Worlds in Austria – track in Vienna, road in Salzburg a week later – we were given Adidas tracksuits and we got to use the same Mavic disc wheels as the senior squad. Anna and I were the only women selected, but there was a men's team-pursuit quartet in a track squad that included Jason Kenny, who went on to win gold medals at Beijing, London and Rio. There were no expectations other than to have fun, but the whole team was successful: Anna won medals – silver in the sprint, bronze in the keirin – Andy Tennant won the individual pursuit, and the lads took silver in the team pursuit after crashing in the final. When it came to the scratch, I was told to do exactly what I'd done for Anna in Italy, but to do it a lap later, and do it for myself. I hit the front hard with a lap and a half to go, and no one came round me until a centimetre from the line. I didn't lunge for it – I didn't know how to – which meant I won silver behind Skye Lee Armstrong of Australia, rather than perhaps a gold.

The road race didn't go quite so well. I was riding well over my limit in a high-class field, and swallowed a fly while going up the main climb. I choked on it, and was bundled into an ambulance, although it wasn't life-threatening. My German wasn't up to explaining to the ambulance men that I wasn't having a seizure, and I wound up in hospital. I wanted out of there; the road team manager John Herety wanted me out too, but the ward nurse – a determined lady who was a cross between Mrs Doubtfire and The Trunchbull in *Matilda* – wasn't having any of it because there were tests that had to be done. So once John had cleared it with my parents, because I was still under-18, he smuggled me out of the ward down a fire escape and we went for an ice cream.

Of all the medals and trophies that I've won, the silver from the scratch race in Vienna is still one that means the most. I was so delighted about it, and the whole team seemed happy, even though it was just a silver. The pleasure began with the fact that I had no idea I was capable of winning anything: I had still not even ridden the British national championships. As in Italy, being with the team felt like a holiday camp: I had no inkling of what stress was at a bike race. The atmosphere in GB was a long way from how it feels today, when there is more pressure, and the whole set-up feels more professional. Winning a medal simply marked a good end to the holiday.

* * *

I had had various ideas about what to do when I left school. I wanted to be a barrister at one point: I didn't really know what it was or what it involved, but I thought that would make me rich. I also considered becoming a policewoman, until I did my work experience alongside a school sports co-ordinator. He worked across the region's schools, making sports accessible to all of them. That meant running school sports days for two weeks solid in between organising leadership awards. I loved it, and I thought maybe that would be a career for me.

What had never entered my head was becoming a professional athlete. At that time I still didn't really appreciate cycling as a sport and my parents still thought it was a hobby. I liked being good at it. I was happy being out on my bike, but I was far from being a cycling fan. I'd never watched the Tour de France on television, because I still preferred netball. Even when I'd got that medal in the Worlds, making a career out of it was still far from being something I contemplated. I just knew I liked the feeling of winning, and I wanted more of that.

CHAPTER 3

FINDING MY FEET

I gradually learnt that there are ways you do certain things as a cyclist, and other things you don't do. Take pinning on race numbers, for example. Perfectly simple, you might think. I'd been to running races with my parents, so I would pin the number to my jersey through the pre-made holes in the corners where there was usually beading to protect the number from the pin. But that wasn't the way a cyclist should do it. I was pinning it on 'like a runner', which meant it would flap in the wind, acting like a brake and slowing me down. At a certain point in the initiation process I was given the 'pinning your number on like a cyclist' talk: you had to put the pins through the fabric of the number to hold it more closely to your jersey, ignoring the pre-made holes, and you had to use more than one pin down each side to make sure that it wouldn't flap. You had to do that while leaving room to get into your pockets to pull out food and without putting a pin through the pocket. And you did it before you put the jersey on, rather than getting someone else to do it when you were wearing it.

It was Phil West who explained which way the pins should go through the numbers. Westy was my first cycling 'parent', and even now, more than ten years on, he remains one of the few people in cycling in whom I would place my trust. He's good with old ladies, a bit funny, a bit of a charmer. Westy is ten years older than me, and had been a good bike rider himself, particularly on the track. He can read a race really well and is a great tactician, who stopped racing because it didn't quite work out for him. After his career ended, he decided to stay in the sport rather than disappear.

As I went upwards through the British Cycling system, Westy was to be my guide to its inner workings. Having been there himself as a rider, he worked for them after quitting racing, but never went back the heart of the team as a coach. He had struggled to play the game there, and he never quite slotted into the British Cycling programme for the same reasons that it never quite seemed to chime with me; he was always on the outskirts. As I came to deal with British Cycling more and more, he knew exactly what was going on and could prepare me for the kind of situations I had to face there. The key difference is that Westy listens a lot more than most coaches. The other coaching relationships I have had since were with British Cycling track coaches, which tended to feel much more like a teacher–student relationship. With Westy it's always been totally different: a conversation between two adults.

Unfortunately, once I turned junior and hit sixth form, school began to feel like the opposite. At GCSE I had managed two A-stars, four As and two Bs. I had hit a good standard, but I had been slipping back a little even then, starting out in set one in maths, then dropping to set two, and the same thing happened in science. I probably wasn't working as hard as I had when I first started school, and when A-levels came around I simply didn't want to be there. I started out doing English, biology, PE and history, but then I dropped English and biology and changed to business, PE and history. I quit English as early as the second lesson, when we were asked to analyse a poem and find the metaphors in it. I was arguing about the poem from a logical standpoint, while the other students spent an hour describing metaphors, which all seemed a bit too obvious. Perhaps I was tired from a training session or perhaps I was playing devil's advocate for the sake of it. Either way, it was frustrating and it wasn't for me, so I left.

At school, I didn't like being treated like a kid, because in my mind I was an adult. I wasn't very good with the rules, which seemed petty. One day I was late for class after lunch, so I took my roller blades to school – the way there was downhill, so that meant I would get there faster – but because I had been seen going through the school grounds on the roller blades, I received a telling off and a detention. That really frustrated me; I was unable to ride my bike that week, and all because I had been trying to get to school on time. I began to struggle with the whole thing: I didn't like having to be there pretending to respect people who I felt didn't deserve it, and I just didn't get on with some of my teachers.

In one school report, Mrs Kendall, my tutor, said she had to stick up for me on many occasions to different members of staff. But it didn't feel as if any of them respected what I was trying to do on my bike and that frustrated me. Teachers seemed to inhabit a small world where school was the most important thing. Here I was going off to Italy, doing the European championships, riding the Worlds, and here they were trying to tell me that my course work about something that I felt was pointless was more important. At times, sixth form felt almost like a kind of popularity contest: members of staff seemed to favour certain kids and not give others as much attention. I remember thinking that when I left school I was never going to come back to one, which is ironic, because after I finish cycling, I may well end up being a teacher. I eventually made a choice: if I thought the teacher was a bad one I wouldn't go to their lessons and I would go out on my bike instead.

The last of my Lottery money went on a holiday in Crete in October 2005 with my friends Beth and Charlotte, although

I did take my bike so I was motivated to train. The week in Crete's main party town of Malia cost us £160 each, in a grotty hotel that was totally empty. We couldn't work out why, until we found out that a woman had been thrown over the balcony by her boyfriend the week before. The training I did there was ridiculous: we would go out until three in the morning when Charlotte and Beth would walk me home so I could get some sleep. They would then go back out until 6am and I would go out later on my bike.

I was training hard, and still playing hockey alongside cycling, but that winter I received a wake-up call when I caught glandular fever and had to have my tonsils out. The holiday in Crete probably contributed to it, although glandular fever is caused by a powerful virus. You shouldn't train with it – you have to give your body a chance to rest and fight the virus. I ended up feeling shattered all the time: I would get in from school and go to sleep before trying to do the turbo session that was on my training programme. And then I would go back to sleep. Eventually my dad took the bike out of the garage and put it in the loft: I was not allowed to ride it again until I recovered. This was an instance where I feel relieved I was in a non-cycling family. Their priority was for me to get better, rather than thinking, 'Wow, the coach from British Cycling is telling her she has to train.' They had sufficient distance to ask me what on earth I was doing.

The lesson wasn't just that I needed to look after myself.

This was one of the first episodes that made me aware that I couldn't necessarily be confident that the people I was working with had my best interests at heart. Even though I had glandular fever I was still being told to train: 'Just keep ticking away, ride your bike a little bit, make sure you can ride so you can come to this training camp in half term', that kind of thing. But I was only seventeen. I wasn't a professional. I was still at school.

It took roughly three months to get through it. Luckily my local doctor had a son who was a very good triathlete – he was our family doctor for years, his sporty son meant he understood athletes, so he guided my recovery. You can only train when you are clear of the glandular fever virus, so I would go and have my blood tests with him and he would say whether I still had it. Even when I was clear at last, I was definitely below par: I wasn't as strong as I had been before.

The illness had one positive outcome: it taught me a lot about listening to my body, how far I could push myself and how much extra recovery I needed. When you are post-viral, you have to be much more careful to recuperate fully after training, so I would be looking for tiredness after my rides. If I felt too tired to go cycling, I would try to recognise that as fatigue, rather than worrying that I was being lazy. Recovery was about learning to differentiate between the two; it's a key lesson that you have to learn as an athlete.

As an organisation, British Cycling hadn't been great during this time: there wasn't enough real care. I wasn't their priority. You could argue that it should have been important for British Cycling to make sure that I was recovering properly, but I don't think they saw it that way. I'm not sure that this had anything to do with my being a girl; I would say it was because I was a junior: I wasn't that high up the pecking order. Luckily, I had Westy on the end of the phone and my family at home saying that I should back off. When I had my tonsils out at the same time, Westy came to visit me in hospital. He was very good throughout that period. It was reassuring to have somebody to turn to who didn't doubt my ability or my talent but who understood the importance of my recovery.

I wouldn't say people are born to be this or that – that always seems a bit extreme – but Westy is made for coaching. He was pretty young to be in that role when I first came across him, taking groups of riders away on camp as a 25-year-old lad, but he was impressive with the logistics of it and also because the camps were good fun. He just seemed to have a way of bringing out the best in people. As a coach, he is better at working with the mental side of cycling than with the physical conditioning side – he's more an amateur psychologist than a physiologist. In my early years, that was what I needed – someone who was quite full-on in that area, to make up for the fact that I didn't have a cycling background.

Early on, I probably needed more help than the other kids around me plus I was going to the junior world championships while the other kids in Otley weren't – so Westy was the person I spoke to most of the time. It was him and his wife Cara who would help me out; Westy took me to the Cheshire Classic when I was a first-year junior, because he knew my mum and dad couldn't make it. He and Cara drove me to a stage race, the Bedford Three-Day, later on in the season. I know other coaches had said to Westy, 'your relationship with Lizzie is too close', but I didn't understand quite what they meant. It's only recently that I asked my dad, 'Did you never think it was strange, because Westy was a 25-year-old lad?' But working with him never felt uncomfortable in any way. In fact, I found it quite insulting when it became clear that other coaches or riders felt my relationship with Westy was 'too close'.

Throughout my career, defining the line between a professional vs. a personal relationship with my coach or manager has been difficult. Coaching relationships are often contentious, whether it's a male coach working with female athletes or a male coach with male athletes. Sadly, there are relatively few women who coach. But coaches will develop closer relationships with some athletes than with others. It's not favouritism, at least not consciously – it's more whether an athlete and a coach 'click' and end up working together in a way that is open, honest and productive.

When you are describing to someone every day in detail how you are feeling both physically and mentally it is inevitable that you will develop a close relationship. I soon came to the conclusion that in sport people will talk about relationships as much as failures and successes. It mattered immensely to me what Phil's wife Cara thought about us working together, that she understood we were working closely together as rider and coach and was happy with that; she was the only one who could have had the right to question the relationship. I could not have any influence over what other people's opinion was, and therefore it was irrelevant.

When I moved on to the second year of the junior programme, British Cycling wanted me to be looked after by the junior podium coach Darren Tudor, so I wasn't officially allowed to work with Westy any more. Darren was coaching the lads' pursuit team and I was peripheral to that. It's not that he isn't a good person or coach, I just wasn't at the top of his to-do list. You could turn it around the other way and say, 'Shouldn't I have been their priority?' But that wasn't the situation. Partly, my family and I weren't keeping on Darren's case: I didn't have parents who were ringing him up and chasing him for training programmes. And I wasn't calling him up, either; I just got on with my cycling.

However, the kind of working relationship I had with Westy is not going to disappear overnight, so he turned into more of a friend and mentor. He no longer gave me training programmes and became more of a sounding board: I would call him and say, 'This session's not going very well, what do you think, should I do something different?' That's how we have worked together ever since. I still struggle to take advice from people who haven't been there and done it, which is why I now like working with Danny Stam at Boels-Dolmans. Danny was a world-class track rider so I trust his advice and direction. He's the only other coach along with Westy who has really brought out the best in me.

* * *

In racing terms, 2006 was about going back to the Europeans in Athens and the Junior Worlds in Ghent and attempting to improve on what I had managed the previous year. It was an eye-opener: I didn't repeat my medal of the year before, but landed two fourth places at both championships. I don't particularly buy into the old cliché that fourth is the unhappiest placing you can get: second is worse. However these were the first goals that I had failed to achieve, the first time I had properly failed in my own eyes. Unlike the previous year when I took everything as it came, the second time around I had actually trained. Even so, I had perspective on it: I'd had that bad winter where I had had tonsillitis and glandular fever, and by that point I already knew I had been accepted on to the British Cycling academy programme so it wasn't the end of the world. I was fourth among my peers and it was pretty cool to be able to say that.

In Ghent, however, my parents and grandparents were at the track. I remember feeling as if I had let them all down because they had actually come to watch this time. They couldn't understand that this year Great Britain had changed from the previous year's holiday-camp atmosphere to being far more serious. If you go to a junior world championships, all the Australians, for example, will sit in the crowd supporting each other even if they have an event the next day. The members of the Great Britain team, on the other hand, were starting to act like senior athletes. I would see my parents in the stadium, give them a wave and then head off to the team hotel. They couldn't work out why this was, because other riders would be sat with their mums and dads having a fun time, while we would be heading off straight away. It reflected the fact that cycling was becoming more popular in the UK, which meant there was more money being put into the team; British Cycling was becoming more professional and that trickled down from the top. In short, the seniors were getting more serious, so the juniors were getting less frivolous.

For 2007, there were three of us in the senior women's academy who were still at school completing our A levels: Katie Curtis, Joanna Rowsell and me. This was handy because we were all fully committed to finishing our exams, whereas a couple of years later, girls would start leaving school in order to go to the academy. Dan Hunt was the coach in charge – later he would go on to run the GB men's endurance squad in London, and he then moved on to become head of performance at the Premier League.

Dan was one of the best coaches in terms of his scientific knowledge and I respected the training he was giving me. He could train me really well; he definitely gave me the best coaching programmes, but he wasn't as direct as I like the people working with me to be. I want to be presented with things in black and white, all the cards out on the table. I didn't feel like we built a real trust between us.

I spent 2007 alternating between school and cycling. Every holiday I had from school would be spent on a training camp, either in Manchester or in Newport. Once school was over, I spent the summer racing in Belgium, where British Cycling had set us up with a team called Global, which was run by Stefan Wyman. Stef is a fixture in British bike racing. His wife Helen is a cyclo-cross racer – she's been British champion many times, and taken medals at the Worlds and Europeans – and Stef has run a British road team for a number of years. He always manages to pull a budget and a sponsor together and gives young British women an opportunity to have a summer race programme.

Global had all sorts of little sponsors: the jersey was full of names, although I didn't recognise any of them. The other girls had sponsored team bikes, but Katie, Jo and I kept riding our Treks because we were on the British Cycling programme. None of the girls were paid but they were provided with accommodation in Belgium in a team house, and race entries and other expenses would be looked after. If I had chosen to road race full-time at this point, Global would have been a good team for me to stay with. I would have been given the opportunity to do some decent races where I would hopefully have been spotted by a bigger team with a more generous budget.

I never had any issues with Stef but there were women who ended up falling out with him. He is very direct and would tell you exactly how something was, which is the approach that suits me. We would have long post-race meetings in which we would dissect what had happened and be told what we had done wrong. I don't know if it is particular to women's teams, but I have often found team meetings frustrating. There are too many times when directors are too scared to rock the boat; they don't want to say anything in case somebody gets upset or takes it the wrong way. My view is that we are professional cyclists who are paid to do a job. Even when I wasn't getting paid I always saw it as a professional affair: it follows that if you are not doing your job properly then you should be told. You can't help feeling that some people believe cycling is their hobby and they are giving their best to be there; for this reason they find it hard to be criticised.

I loved being in Belgium: we stayed in a house in Tielt-Winge, which is to the east of Brussels in the province of Brabant. The house was one of several that Tim Harris, a British guy who had raced as a pro, and his partner Jos, would rent out to teams. There was me, Jo and Katie, Stef and Helen, a lad called Dino, and Gabby Day, another cyclo-cross rider, plus whoever would come and go from the team. It was basic accommodation: as many beds as they could fit in each bedroom; bunk beds and one washing machine between however many of us there happened to be; and a cooking and cleaning rota. We would do all the chores for ourselves.

Katie, Jo and I were finding our feet, just the three of us, and it was always quirky. We had been thrown together and made a strange trio; in fact, we probably wouldn't have been friends if it hadn't been for cycling, but we made it work. We were all very different: Jo was still very shy and quiet at that time – she would later go on to become a mainstay of the GB women's pursuit team, winning gold in the London and Rio Games – while Katie was a clever bike rider, a good racer, but I think she found it overwhelming. She had been a really talented junior but I suspect she struggled with the workload as a senior and the independence that it all demanded.

It was a very different world, like going back in time: we didn't even have the Internet. Jo was the only one who had a laptop, and she had DVDs, which we would watch on the little screen. I used the phone in the team house to call home rather than my mobile, which was too expensive. Most of all, I remember being hungry. That ran through it all the time: always wanting more to eat. We didn't have enough money to cater generously, and we didn't have a car between us, so we had to wait to buy food until Stef and Helen decided they wanted to go to the supermarket. We would go with them and then there would be a house allowance given to each of us, but I would always want to eat more than my ration. It didn't get to me particularly, but the next time I went I made sure I took a food bag, with plenty to eat in it.

As for the racing, I liked it and it seemed to suit me. Early on, we raced at the Omloop van Borsele in south-west Netherlands – a totally flat race which always breaks up into echelons. I came fifth in a small group behind Kirsten Wild and everyone was saying how good it was. I didn't really realise quite how strong a ride it was for a first-year senior, but Stef and Helen said it was pretty impressive.

There were good and bad days, and the cat day was one that sticks in the mind. To start with, I don't like cats – in fact, I am scared of animals. I don't buy the idea that they are fluffy and cute or cuddly. My mum is scared of dogs and so am I, and our next-door neighbours in Otley had cats that I avoided. I wasn't lucky when it came to pets either: my brother and sister had guinea pigs but they went missing. My brother had a hamster but it went crazy and started biting people. What happened in Tielt-Winge didn't make me any better disposed towards them. We had only one washing machine, which was shared on a rota. I had washed my kit, someone had taken it out of the washing machine and left it in the basket for me to hang up. When I got to it, I thought, 'this stinks', and I then realised that a cat had pissed all over my jersey and shorts. I still had to race in it, because it was the only kit I had.

There were other episodes straight out of the book of things that shouldn't happen to a cyclist. Take that year's Tour of Brittany, which was a stage race ranked 2.2 (so not the highest level – one below with club teams as well as a pro squad) by the UCI, so it wasn't a major race. We stayed in schools in between the stages, and as riders we just weren't prepared for what that involved. Ten years on, if I was travelling to a race like that I'd know to take lots of my own food, some good pyjamas and probably a pillow. In fact, I probably just wouldn't contemplate riding that particular race: the schools we were lodged in doubled up as summer camps, and we were given meal tickets and slept on camp beds positioned between school desks for some privacy. That made it a test of endurance on and off the bike.

At the end of the race we were dropped off at a Formula One hotel where we had to share a room between the three of us. Formula One hotels are famously basic, so there was the usual bunk bed and a double bed and not much else. We were tired and hungry and, inevitably, we had an argument about which two of us were going to have to share the double bed. Then we went out for dinner. The Formula One was plonked down by itself out by a main road, so we had to walk along the highway to get to dinner, skinny and starving. Then came the final body blow: we had no euros on us. Luckily Jo had a credit card so she paid for us all; she wasn't exactly delighted, but Katie and I didn't have cards.

On another occasion we flew into Brussels airport after a race, we got in the taxi and we said to the driver we wanted to go to Tielt-Winge. Unfortunately he took us to a different Tielt-Winge, on the opposite side of Belgium, and then did his utmost to charge us 300 euros for the ride. Inevitably, it was Jo who sorted it out, in the way that she fixed most things in those early days. It was Jo who always seemed to end up our saviour. She usually had a bit of cash about her, and in contrast to me and Katie, she always seemed to have a good idea of where we were.

CHAPTER 4

PULL YOUR HEAD IN

My first taste of road racing in the proper sense, of big events in Europe, came in 2007. I began to like it. It was too early to say that I preferred road racing to track, because the track was still my priority, but I couldn't help seeing the principal appeal of the road: freedom. Road racing was less controlled than the track, both in the way you trained, and – compared to the team pursuit at least – in the way you would race and the way you would live. The road involved more travel, took you to different places, and there was a bigger circle of people to rub shoulders with.

That summer I was selected for the world road-race championships, which were to be held in Stuttgart in September; this was quite something for a first-year senior.

It meant a four-day training camp in Italy – in Quarrata where the GB men's under-23 academy was based – with all the senior girls, overseen by the Welsh coach Julian Winn, a former road professional. He was to manage the Great Britain women's road team in the run-in to Beijing, where Nicole Cooke was to win gold.

I have never had role models in cycling; when people ask me I've always found the question difficult because I came into cycling late and I ended up competing against the people who would have been the ones to emulate. As a racer, you don't want to put those people on a pedestal. But when I started cycling and I was doing my turbo sessions I did have a poster of Nicole on my garage door. You couldn't help being aware of her: the British men racing on the road weren't that good at the time, whereas Nicole was the best in the world and she was basically doing it on her own.

Nicole seemed so focused, so driven. We sat down to dinner in the hotel in Quarrata, and this guy turned up; he had two sets of wheels with him. Nicole got up from the table, took the wheels off him and sat back down. We asked, 'Who was that?'

'That's my boyfriend – he just brought my wheels.'

He had driven five hours or something to bring her these wheels and she didn't seem fazed by it. She had an unbelievable amount of what I can only describe as killer instinct, and she trained hard, very hard. I remember thinking: 'God, how am going to last the week?'

Nicole is five years older than me, from South Wales, born into a cycling family. She had been an incredible competitor since her early years, taking three junior world championships in 2001: road, time trial, mountain bike. She was in her prime at this point: she had won medals in the road Worlds three times in the previous four years, although she had yet to win a senior gold; she had taken a string of one-day Classics and won the World Cup three times, she was ranked number one in the world and had taken six national road titles on the trot.

I found Nicole incredibly direct. We would sit in team meetings and she would seem to speak more than the manager. As a team leader, she would tell you what your job in a race was but she would also take the time to explain your role. She was utterly confident. She oozed self-belief. She would go into a race wanting it to be hard, and wanting her team to make it tough for everyone else. That put her on a different level as far as I was concerned. I remember thinking, 'Why do you want it to be hard? Surely you want it to be as easy as possible.' Now I understand why she wanted racing to be demanding for her opponents, but I only cottoned on once I began to become competitive at the highest level.

With the senior women I went on from Italy to a stage race at Albstadt in Germany, where I came down with food poisoning. It was bad enough for me to be hospitalised when I got back home, but this was another instance where

I wasn't given enough time to recover by the Great Britain team: there always seemed to be pressure on me to get back in shape for the next race without properly giving myself time to get healthy. Again my family and friends had to step in.

I got over the illness in time for Stuttgart, where Nicole didn't make the team due to a knee injury that required surgery; without her, Emma Pooley was our strongest rider. The first thing that struck me about the Worlds was how hard it was. It was a massive shock. I was used to racing 80 kilometres and this was 140. I remember seeing Giorgia Bronzini, who was to win the Worlds in 2010 and 2011, and thinking 'Wow!' She had legs that looked just like pistons. There were climbs on the course that were like nothing I had ever climbed even in training: the Birkenkopf and the Herdweg, which was really steep – 14 per cent – around 700 metres long, and like a wall. And there was the long drag to the finish. 'Oh my God,' I thought.

My job was to last as long as possible and to be on the front on one particular descent every lap. I remember dropping other riders on that descent – I wouldn't do that these days, but when I was a younger rider I was happier to take risks than I am now. Each time round, I would have an advantage on the field as we went through the more technical part of the course, so back home in front of the television, my granddad thought I was winning. Obviously, I wasn't: I lasted three of the seven laps. I couldn't really expect much more of myself; that year I had just finished A levels and it was the first summer I had spent riding consistently on the road. The team management thought I had done a good job, so they were happy; Emma finished tenth, proving that at last there was a second British woman of world standard alongside Nicole.

That autumn I moved to Manchester to join the British Cycling academy, where I was to share a flat with Anna Blyth; she had kicked on from our junior days to win the European under-23 keirin title that year, and had got close to a medal at the senior Worlds. The flat was a basic two bedroom in Fallowfield, the Manchester suburb where the GB academy flats were; it's not the nicest part of the world, but Anna was a great housemate. I owe most of my happy memories from Manchester to her. I spent a bit of money in IKEA to try to make my very clinical room more comfortable and cosy; Anna did the same with hers.

The academy was hard work: it comes at a point in your career where you are turning into a full-time athlete but you are also learning to live independently. I was lucky that at home I had already done a lot of things for myself, so I could cook and clean, but budgeting was a novelty: our grant was £6,000, but £3,000 was taken off us directly to pay for rent; the rest had to cover our upkeep and everything else. Mum and Dad supplemented this with an extra £20 a week. It doesn't sound like a lot but it made a crucial difference when doing the weekly food shop; Anna and I would drive in her Mini Cooper to the local Morrisons, our favourite supermarket.

At the women's academy it was the same three riders as before – Katie, Jo and me – but in Manchester we were integrated with the senior women's programme because, unlike the under-23 men, there weren't enough of us to justify a programme of our own. The disparity was obvious: the men's academy had their own coach, their own programme and would go to Italy to race all summer after riding the track in Manchester through the winter.

Along with the two senior women – Wendy Houvenaghel and Rebecca Romero – we were all being coached by Dan Hunt, who had looked after us the previous winter. Jo and I slotted into the women's programme straight away but Katie didn't last very long due to illness and other issues.

For Great Britain, 2008 would be about the Beijing Olympics. I had been put on the long-list as a potential member of the road-race team, while the points race, one of my specialities, was still an Olympic event. For that year, along with most of the women riding for GB at the time, I joined the Halfords-Bikehut team, which had been set up largely as a vehicle to enable Nicole to prepare for the Olympics and supplied us with a bike and kit. Emma Pooley stuck with her Specialized team, but Jo, Wendy, Katie and I were among the ones to join up, because whether or not we made it to Beijing we would need a team to do whatever racing we ended up with – Belgian kermesses or the European events alongside Nicole.

I was just behind that Olympic group, so I didn't work with Julian Winn closely, but he was a hands-on coach, and – together with Simon Cope, then in charge of the junior women – he was one of the few coaches I have seen over the years who have adopted the role of looking after the GB women who has grasped it with both hands and enjoyed it. Whether he did the job well or not I never personally found out – he was moved on at the end of 2008 – but Julian clearly liked it, which was valuable. He actually wanted to do it – it was more than a case of, 'Oh, you take charge of the girls for the weekend.'

Jo made it into the GB team for the inaugural world team pursuit championship in Manchester in April along with Rebecca and Wendy; there, I managed seventh in the scratch behind Ellen Van Dijk and 19th in the points race behind Marianne Vos. My chances of making it to Beijing went west in the spring, when I picked up a back injury, related to saddle issues, which meant an operation and ten weeks out of racing. I went under the knife on 1 May, but in any case, a strong candidate had emerged for the third place in the women's road-race team alongside Nicole and Emma: Sharon Laws, who joined Halfords that April, and would eventually join them in Beijing.

I did make it to an Olympic training camp that spring, where Sharon broke her foot in a freak accident when she

71

fell off her bike while we were filming in the Cotswolds with some media. We had been asked to do race simulations for a documentary – Sharon and Emma Trott had been told to attack up the road, and when we turned a corner we saw Sharon on the floor. I remember thinking it was ridiculous – it was wet, it was cold and I couldn't work out what we were doing it for.

Whereas the others would moan to each other about the sessions being too difficult or ineffective due to the bad weather, I would always voice my opinions to the coaches. I often find myself in this position, speaking out on behalf of teammates and then finding I have little support at crunch time. The response was often 'pull your head in', that sort of thing, in other words, keep quiet and get on with it. It was one of Dan Hunt's favourite sayings: he was probably right on some occasions.

Once I'd got over the operation, Jo and I went back to Tim Harris and Jos Ryan's at Tielt-Winge, to ride kermesses. For that summer, while Julian Winn oversaw the senior team as they built towards Beijing with Nicole, we were being looked after by Simon Cope, the junior women's coach, who was also based in Belgium, with riders like Katie Colclough, Hannah Mayho, Lucy Martin and Alex Greenfield, who were about to form the next academy intake.

Jo and I were racing in the UK on 10 August when Nicole won the road race; I remember someone on the side of the road shouted the result at us. We were all delighted although, ironically, I thought of myself as a track rider so I was more interested in the track results than what was happening on the road, where Emma took silver in the time trial to back up Nicole's gold. In that context, I landed one significant result that summer: in Belgium the week before Beijing, Jo and I rode a kermesse where I made it into the winning break with Emma Johansson and then beat her in the sprint. Emma went on to take the silver medal behind Nicole in Beijing.

Jo and I had a whale of a time that summer; ours is a friendship that has endured, to the point where I would say she is my only real friend in cycling, the only friend I have who completely understands my job. That may have its roots in the fact that I was probably the first person who saw beyond Jo's alopecia. I was the first person who spoke to her about it; that is how I had been brought up – to be direct. I said to her directly: 'What is the story?' Nobody really seemed to understand it; people tended to do that British thing where you think, 'Oh, got to be tactful, mustn't talk about that.' It was a lovely summer for her and me because she came out of her shell completely and totally changed. She started out very shy and a bit of a swot – she would have her head in a book all the time – and I think she was thrown into a situation with me where she had no choice but to communicate.

Jo and I were – are – very different. Jo went to an all girls' school and her plan was to be an A-star student. You would never have expected her to become what she is now, the stalwart of the team-pursuit team, the only member to have stayed the course since the very beginning as they have gone on to take one world title after another and that Olympic gold in London. She was terribly shy, but she was determined and committed and I like that about her. With all her power, she is also made for the team pursuit: she has always been one of the strongest riders GB has had.

You can be typecast very quickly in cycling. Early on Jo was put down as a 'diesel': powerful but with not a huge amount of skill. If these labels are attached to you early in your career and reiterated time and again you start to believe it and as a result, Jo can be a nervous bike handler. That's something that has frustrated me over the years, because she is actually more skilful than people give her credit for.

There was one kermesse the following year that we had entered along with the GB academy girls managed by Simon Cope; we had ridden there from Tim's house. I said to Jo at the start that we could win – it was a tight circuit of the kind I love – so we attacked together and built a big lead fairly rapidly. I was full of confidence, delighted that we were showing everyone how to race aggressively. I threw my bike into one tight left-hand corner with Jo on my wheel, but unfortunately there were three different kinds of asphalt on the apex of the turn and I overcooked it, bringing Jo down with me in a tangle of bodies and bikes. Even more annoyingly, we fell right in front of Simon. He was under the impression we had been pushing each other too hard and was absolutely livid. That couldn't have been further from the truth: we were friends working together to prove him wrong.

* * *

The world road-race championship in the north Italian town of Varese at the end of that season was pretty intense. I had split up with Adam – the first of hundreds of times – and he had moved to South Africa for seven weeks. It was my first experience of heartbreak, or whatever you want to call it, and I had lost a lot of weight. I remember getting to Varese and sitting next to Chris Froome. It was his first Worlds as a British national; he seemed like a nice, sweet guy and very quiet. Nicole came into it off the back of her Olympic gold medal – she was riding close to her home in Switzerland – and she would be one of the favourites.

I was told to cover moves in the beginning of the race; the first four laps would be my responsibility. I ended up getting into an early break of a dozen riders, with all the big nations in there apart from the Netherlands and Switzerland, which lasted for seven of the eight laps of the race. I just knew I had to stay there; it was so hard with two climbs each lap, Montello and Ronchi. With Nicole in the bunch waiting to make her move, we didn't want the break to stay away to the finish, but we wanted the Dutch to have to spend energy controlling it. I wasn't allowed to do a turn, which meant I was getting shouted at by the other women in the break – it is quite intimidating when you have an Olympic champion like Kristin Armstrong yelling at you – and Shane Sutton was on the side of the road shouting instructions to stay where I was and not work. The break got caught just before the first climb on the final circuit. Nicole came up to me and I said, 'What can I do? What can I do?'

'You have to attack up this climb.'

I gave it a big push on the last climb, Nicole countered and went on to win the sprint from a five-rider group including Johansson and Vos. I came in 41st, five minutes back.

As usual, Nicole had been completely confident before-hand. Emma had taken a silver medal in Beijing, where she had ridden strongly in the road race before Nicole made her move, but there was never any question of GB having dual leadership: this was Nicole's race. As a pair, they are totally different. Emma doesn't ooze confidence, she is quite insecure and timid, and she is very intelligent, almost too intelligent to be a bike rider. She was always concerned about what everyone else was thinking and whether everyone else in the team was all right. It got to the point where I found this frustrating: if you take good care of yourself, then I have a better chance of taking care of you.

Emma had a decent shout of winning the Worlds in later years, notably at Mendrisio in 2009, but in my opinion she suffered from a lack of astute team management, which

bove: Christmas Day with my mum. I am exactly a week old.

elow: A typical Sunday walk with my brother, Nick; we're probably enjoying it despite urselves.

Above: Enjoying one of Mum's infamous 'budget picnics' after sneaking in through the back gate at Harewood House.

Below: One of our family holidays… Adventures and holidays were always a priority!

Left: Washing my new bike – a memorable Christmas and the first one I used after stabilisers.

Below: My mum has saved a ton of press cuttings of my races over the years. Here's one of me smiling proudly alongside my cousin Sam after we became the youngest competitors in the local river race.

.....Athletics, Bowls, Golf, Swimming

Sam Dunn and Lizzie Armitstead (pictured left) were the youngest finishers in the Otley River Race Ages ranged from six years to over 40 and it was a real family affair.

Town Mayor Ray Dunn swam in the event as well as presenting the prizes and he was joined in the race by his son Graham, daughter-in-law Karen, seven year-old grandson Sam and Karen's mother Janet Renshaw.

Five members of the Cherry family took part as did three of the Woods.

Ben Riley was the race winner in 5 mins 32 secs with Graham Dunn second and Tom Hawley third. Cathy Allen won the ladies' race in 6 mins 10 secs with Karen Dunn second and Lisa Cherry third.

Above: One of the last holidays Nick and I went on with our parents. We had out-grown the camping holidays in France and certainly needed our own space by that age!

Below: In the early days of training, my dad would teach me new routes and give me a good run for my money!

Below: Fresh-faced and excited for the Junior European Championships in Athens with Katie Curtis.

Left: Proudly holding onto my Silver Scratch race medal. I survived a last-minute crash but managed to sustain some nerve damage in my little finger.

© *Getty Images*

Above: In full flight and feeling great at the 2009 Track World Championships.

Below: A standard setting for the start of a Women's Giro stage… you quickly learn how to make a car park your changing room.

Above: Mum and Dad, who had come to support me at the Women's Tour. It is always so nice when I get the chance to combine racing and family.

Below: My Grandma chatting to Mike from BP at the London Olympics. As you can see, she is always wearing her yellow T-shirt at races.

Left: A photo taken on my mobile phone as I looked up to cross the road on Oxford Street: I was in shock to see the image of myself on the side of Adidas. A pinch-me moment.

Great Britain

#takethestage

adidas

Right: A photo booth set up in the Adidas kitting-out shop before London 2012 was a popular place to show off your new kit and funny faces!

stemmed from the fact that the Great Britain women's team has never had a team manager who worked consistently alongside us for any length of time. We never had a manager who would lead a team meeting knowing Emma's character enough to give her the boost to her ego that she needed, by saying straight up, 'Emma, this race: you can win it.' Instead, team managers would sit there and say, 'Emma, I know that you are scared on the descents but just sit near the front and you will be OK.' She didn't need to hear that because she is a good descender, and she shouldn't have been scared going downhill, but if some stranger has a preconceived idea of who you are as a rider and reinforces that in a team meeting when you are already on the edge of it all falling apart, it isn't going to help. I saw this every year and it was incredibly frustrating.

Personally, I loved Varese. I did a good job. I was on television. My family watched it; they all thought it was really cool. I had just come through a bad experience in my personal life so I felt quite vulnerable and then it turned: I felt I was going well and that was a massive, massive boost to my confidence. It's not the only time I've found that when I have challenges in my life, when things aren't that straightforward, I find it easier to suffer on my bike.

I went from there to the 2008 World Cup in Manchester at the end of October and won the team pursuit with Jo and Katie, riding for the academy, then added the points and the scratch. It was really special: three gold medals, the first I had ever won in the World Cup and in front of a British crowd who were buzzing after our most successful Olympics and a team heaving with stars such as Chris Hoy and Vicky Pendleton. The British women made a clean sweep of every discipline, with Anna taking gold in the team sprint with Jess Varnish. It was particularly satisfying because the women's points race had been the only event where we didn't get a medal in Beijing.

It had seemed bizarre to me that a cyclist might need an agent, and the attention that came my way after the Manchester World Cup was a shock. It was huge, and I didn't know how to handle it. Not long afterwards I was contacted by Jonathan Marks, who runs MTC, where Emma worked. I met him in Manchester. He's a dapper little man, and he came across well. Looking back, I realise he's also smart: to sweeten the negotiations we went to an Adidas shop where I was given a contract, and £500 or something to spend there and then.

That autumn, the girls who had been in the junior academy moved up to senior, which meant there was a new women's under-23 academy run by Simon Cope and based in Manchester in the winter, Belgium in the summer. There were World Cups to race that winter – in Melbourne and Copenhagen, where Katie, Jo and I won the team pursuit both times and I added two more gold medals in the scratch – but most importantly in terms of my career, we went to ride the Amsterdam Six Day the week before the World Cup in Manchester.

In typical British Cycling fashion it was something of a do-it-yourself job: we had to drive to Harwich to take the overnight ferry. It wasn't long since I had passed my test, which I managed second time around in spite of not having formal lessons. As was typical of my mum and dad I had been given a choice: I could pay for driving school or have my parents help me to learn. I tried first with Dad, which was terrible, so I learnt with Mum; I failed on my first attempt but passed on the second in my mum's car, after which – this seems ridiculous now – I drove straight from the test centre to Manchester because I had a training session on the velodrome. I almost killed myself on the motorway because I didn't understand at all how the blind spot worked until I actually got on to the M62. That is how my mum and dad do things; I'm not sure that many parents would let their child loose on the motorway that soon.

Simon took three of the girls to Harwich in a GB team car, and I drove down with Lucy Martin in my Peugeot 306, which was my first car. I'd gone to Leeds with my dad to buy it, £1200 cash in hand, which was a huge amount of money at the time. It had various idiosyncrasies: when I put the indicator on, for some reason the alarm would go off; on top of that, the battery had a tendency to die, so I was worried enough to bring jump leads with me just to be covered. The radio had disappeared when it had been broken into, so Lucy brought speakers with batteries and we listened to her iPod on the way to Harwich.

The Amsterdam Six was good fun, a proper old-school six-day with racing every night until the small hours. The routine was always the same: go out for a ride in the morning, have a sleep all afternoon, wake up and get on the boards until two in the morning. In terms of racing, the demands were pretty similar to the men's: elimination race, scratch, points, with a Madison to close the night. Like the men we had cabins on the edge of the velodrome to change and eat in, with Portakabins out on the side to take refuge in between races; they were freezing but it was good fun.

Alex Greenfield, who had just come up from junior, was my teammate; we won overall, but that wasn't the most significant outcome. For one thing, this was the first time I met Danny Stam, my current team director, who was racing in the event with his regular partner Robert Slippens. Rochelle Gilmore, who now runs the Wiggle-High5 team, was also racing; I bumped into her talking to Dany Schoonbaert, who was the manager of Lotto-Belisol, the Belgian team that I wanted to ride for.

I had a strong winter on the track, fired up by an Adidas contract that promised me bonuses if I won three medals at the world championships held in Pruskov, just outside Warsaw. I earned that bonus thanks to gold in the team pursuit, silver in the scratch and bronze in the points, and I did it all with my grandparents watching from the stands, which was even sweeter. I had a lot to thank Simon Cope for, as his quick thinking was critical in the scratch, where I crashed with six laps to go on the back straight, and was unable to get my foot out of the pedal. Simon ran up the track, forced my foot out, got me to the bottom of the boards, had a quick look at my front wheel, which was broken, and made the split-second call not to change it.

It was a risky decision, but it had to be taken rapidly as there would have been no time to switch the wheel with the finish less than 90 seconds away. So he put me back on a broken bike, but it paid off: I managed silver in the sprint. It did take a while for the commissaires to decide whether I was allowed the medal, as the Italians put in a protest in the hope that they could get Bronzini bumped up from fourth. Finally, the call was made that as the crash happened at six laps to go – just outside the five specified by the rules – the result would stand. The crash left me with nerve damage in my little finger and third finger, from hitting my elbow – it only took a couple of weeks to recover – so I had to race the points race with it strapped up.

There was clearly a future for me on the track with Great Britain if I wanted it, the more so because at this stage the points race was still on the Olympic schedule, but I had other plans centred on the road. Dany Schoonbaert had offered me a contract with Lotto of about a couple of hundred euros a month plus a bike and support at the bigger races, though at smaller events, kermesses and so on, I would have to look after myself. That might not seem great but it's still unusual to get as much as that. I had seen Lotto when I was racing the kermesses that summer and I wanted to ride for them. I knew the GB academy would be based in Flanders as well, in the town of Oudenaarde, but I wanted to be independent of them. In 2009, I wanted to ride for Lotto, live where I wanted to live, and do my own thing.

CHAPTER 5

MAGNUMS, *NACHTWINKELS* AND PETER PAN

The alarm in the Eurotunnel wagon woke me up and reminded me where I was: in Calais. I had dozed off on the train after driving down from Otley in my newly bought Audi A3, which had – fortunately – replaced the Peugeot. The thought of buying that Audi had been a motivating factor in my training all that winter, although I'm not quite sure why as cars are not one of my passions. I suspect it may have been Adam's influence as he liked shiny things – he was a year younger than me and I was in a position to buy it. I don't actually have a car now, just a scooter for zipping around in Monaco.

Dad and I found the car on *Auto Trader* and drove to Tadcaster to have a look at it; we pulled up at the owner's house, to find him polishing the car. Dad got out of our car to shake hands and introduce himself, and after about five minutes of small talk the man explained that he wasn't selling his car at all and we had the wrong house. Unbelievably, we managed to come across another house with an A3 on the drive, only to learn that wasn't the one for sale either; we eventually bought the third one. After I got back from Poland with GB, I packed all my belongings into the Audi and drove to the Tunnel. There I bought a satnav: next stop, Tim Harris and Jos Ryan's house in Stationsstraat, Westmeerbeek, a smallish village east of Brussels in the province of Antwerp.

Perhaps this should have felt like a huge step for me, but it didn't have that sense at the time. I hadn't thought much about the fact that I was going to have to drive in a different country and that this might be a new beginning. I knew where I was going. I knew where Tim and Jos lived. I knew how to drive. What was the big deal? Mainly, I felt relieved to be escaping from Manchester and to be getting away from the British Cycling programme; I was going to have a summer where I would be in control and which I knew I was going to enjoy. I had got back together with Adam – this was to become something of a theme in the next few years, unfortunately – and we rented a room at Tim and Jos's.

At times that spring and summer the four of us were like a weird, dysfunctional family: Tim from Norfolk, Jos from Lancashire, plus two Yorkshire folk. Tim and Adam seemed

almost like best mates although Adam was 19 and Tim was...
well, we don't actually know: he seems like Peter Pan. No
one is certain quite how old he might be. Tim is a former pro
from the 1980s and '90s, a bit of a Del Boy, who owns his
own furniture business, and is constantly heading off here,
there and everywhere to do deals. He'd turn up in his yellow
truck and you'd be thinking, 'What's in the back of it this
time?' The last time I can remember, it was mattresses from
Colombia. He still rides his bike, going through periods of
being fit and less fit with no real difference in speed. He
manages to do random five-hour rides on his bike and still
win the sprint at the end of it even if he has not ridden a
bike for six months. He's a bit of a charmer in his own way,
very warm, very open, very direct, always has a story to tell
and, no matter what the weather, he always has a string vest
under his top.

As well as their own house in Westmeerbeek, Tim and Jos
rented out various other properties, like the one I'd stayed
at in Tielt-Winge: tenants included national teams from
New Zealand and Canada, Stef and Helen Wyman's Global,
sometimes the British men's under-23 academy. Over the
years, they've done a great deal to help a good many people
in cycling, partly through their links to the Dave Rayner
Fund, which supports young riders who want to race abroad.
'The Rayner' is a charity based in Yorkshire, named after a
much-loved professional cyclist from the county who died
young, and tragically.

Belgium was like being in a whole new world, and Tim and Jos were great at helping us integrate into the lifestyle. Apart from their cat, which I loathed, Stationsstraat was a good place to live. We would go for rides with Tim when Tim was home from one of his adventures. So many times they would end up as epic outings. Tim would blow up, getting 'the bonk' when he ran out of fuel: 'Give me one of them gel things, give me one of them gel things,' he would plead. We'd stop at bakeries and sit on the side of the road and down a Coke and a pie or a bun and keep going.

We would always sprint for the town and village signs, week in week out, every ride, barely missing one, and Tim wouldn't think twice about throwing the odd hook when it got competitive. He would really stick his elbow into you. The amount of times we almost crashed seems fairly reckless when I look back now. The one time we actually hit the deck was when Adam had just got selected to ride Paris–Roubaix – serious stuff as a first-year pro – and became overcommitted in one particular sprint. Tim thought it was hilarious. He was laughing his head off. What's certain, however, is that among the risk-taking and the laughter I was constantly learning how to sprint – long sprints, short sprints, uphill, downhill, out of corners, into the wind, in a crosswind – against men who were bigger and stronger, and knew plenty of tricks.

Belgium is so featureless that we always seemed to be on a new road, or at least one we didn't recognise. It is incredibly difficult to find your way on a bike there to begin with because there are no real hills, so you don't ever get a perspective of where you are; all the houses look different and you can be on bike paths that suddenly turn into canals. As a result, we seemed to get constantly lost. But there is such a strong cycling culture – everyone loves it – that if you are ever in trouble on a bike you have only got to wait two minutes before there will be another cyclist along to help you. Once, we rode across a cornfield – 'Why not?' we thought. 'Let's ride through the corn, and see if there is anything on the other side' – and eventually ended up in someone's back garden, where they gave us cheese and wine, just because we had turned up on our bikes.

I would go upstairs, shower, come down to eat and Tim would be sitting there telling us a story about a bottle of wine he might have brought back from Colombia ten years ago. He would be eating cheese and drinking the wine, telling us how brilliant it was, although it tasted awful. Chorizo seemed to play a big part in his life: we would have chorizo risotto all the time and there would always be coffee as well. I was a vegetarian and a non-coffee drinker, and perhaps he found those two things difficult to relate to, but we got on well. I learnt a lot from Tim: he would always encourage a rider, tell you how good you were, and that you could win this sprint or that one.

Belgium was a lovely lifestyle. It was a great experience to go there and become part of it when I was only 20. The locals knew there were young cyclists around, so they would help out when they could. There was one particular cafe where the couple became Lizzie Armitstead supporters to an extent that became a bit overpowering. Cycling is their national sport, and to them you could be the next celebrity – they want to be part of that. We would go to kermesses, get extra prize money in primes and we would care about that, because it would mean we could do nice things; if we were really struggling for money Tim would let us varnish his chairs for a bit of cash. On the way back from races, we'd stop at the *frites* shop and if we had had a good race we would always ride on the town bikes down to the convenience store – they call them the *nachtwinkels* – to buy Magnum ice creams. Then we would sit and eat them and watch TV.

Before every major race, I would drive myself to my team manager's house in Aalst, about an hour and a half away, to travel on to wherever we needed to go. He didn't speak any English, so I would communicate by email through his daughter about when the races were, where I had to be, and when. I've spent my whole career now with Dutch-speaking teams so my Flemish has improved; that was partly thanks to Tim, who encouraged me to learn with phrase books in the house. He speaks his own variant of Flemish with a Norfolk drawl, and also has his own vocabulary in English – he calls everybody 'chap' – and he would keep saying, 'Lizzie you are going to be a *vedette* – a star – to be a *vedette*, you need to do this or you need to do that.'

There was one thing you couldn't miss if you were a cyclist living in Belgium: the importance of the races, which are all centred around the Tour of Flanders. Through the spring, cycling is on television every weekend in what feels like the Christmas build-up, except it's the build-up to Flanders. The countdown of races – Het Nieuwsblad, E3, Gent–Wevelgem – feels like an advent calendar where each weekend you open up a new door: to me Flanders is Christmas Day, the big window on the calendar. It was one of the first men's races to have a women's event alongside it on the same day – it started in 2004 – and the same immense crowds watch both. That makes Flanders the biggest one-day Classic on the women's calendar, in significance and scale, with all the key elements of the men's race, the same climbs and cobbled roads, but leaving out the boring early part: you don't go from the frying pan into the fire; you miss the frying pan out and go straight into the flames. The other major Belgian races for women – Nieuwsblad, Gent–Wevelgem, Flèche Wallonne – follow the same format.

Living with Tim and Jos accentuated the divide I was beginning to sense separating me from the Great Britain team. Our hosts were both a bit anti-establishment: the Dave Rayner Fund was about riders making their way outside the Great Britain system. They were looking after Adam, who had left the GB academy on not the best of terms, and I had made a very conscious choice not to live in Oudenaarde with the other GB girls. Tim advocated total independence for a cyclist because that was the old-school way in which he had had to live and race in order to earn a professional contract himself. So I was going to the kermesses on my own, making my own drink bottles and my own race food, which was a great way to learn the ropes.

I was also beginning to coach myself, which is where it got complicated. I had been working with Dan Hunt all winter, as before, and that summer Simon Cope was looking after the GB academy girls in Belgium. Jo and I never made the transition into that set-up, so we fell between two fences. Jo was still very focused on the track – she was training mainly for the individual pursuit, with UK time trials on top of that. So she was doing pursuit training on the boards throughout the summer and would come out to stay in Belgium with us for few weeks at a time.

That summer she met her future husband, Dan Shand – another British rider racing in Belgium as so many do – and I played my part in that. It was a warm evening, my parents had come over to experience a bit of Belgian bike-riding life, so we all went to Herentals, Rik Van Looy's home town, to watch Adam and Dan ride. On the way home after the race, I took Adam and my parents, and – in full knowledge of what I was possibly setting up – said that 'with the bike in the car' there wasn't enough room for Jo, so she would have to travel with Dan, although she was horrified. They got married in 2015.

In some races, it would almost feel as if it was the two

of us versus the GB academy; there was one kermesse in particular where it was boiling hot, the GB academy was there as well, while I was competing unsupported as a Lotto rider. I had run out of water and as I rode through the feed zone I wanted to take a bottle off a GB staff member; he took it away from me. I thought, 'This is a small race, the temperature's 40 degrees, I am a British rider, help me out.' That's stuck with me.

In 2009, because the team pursuit was yet to be put on the Olympic programme, I was still allowed to focus on the points race, which was still part of the track schedule. From a physical point of view I thought that Dan got the best out of me, but Great Britain was a bizarre environment in some ways. We would go on Majorca training camps where it was quite clear that the senior riders, Wendy Houvenaghel and Rebecca Romero, didn't get on. Their relationship wasn't a role model for me and Jo. On one particular training ride in Majorca, all four of us had just finished a team time trial training session and the idea was to ride home slowly to recover. Unfortunately for Jo and me, Wendy and Rebecca ended up on the front. Neither of them were willing to let the other one dictate the pace; as a result they were half wheeling each other and the pace was getting faster and faster. Eventually me and Jo looked across at each other, broke into a giggle and watched them race off into the Majorcan sunset. I understood that they were going for the same medal and it was pretty intense.

Travelling around Europe with Lotto, there was no such pressure and no politics. I was just finding my feet. I was beginning to love road racing more and more. It was a bigger world than track cycling, which seemed more limited in its scope. The road was constantly exciting. I was part of a team of people who had come from different cultures, girls from all over the world. It was a challenge and I was coming to love it. There were stars here; in fact, there was one big star, Marianne Vos, who I'd first come across when we were juniors. At pretty much every race we went to, if Vos was there, the story was the same: we'd be racing for second.

I have minimal contact with Marianne as we've never been teammates; I respect her, but I can't call her a friend. What I can say is that I've never seen a rider want it as much as she does. She will celebrate a criterium win as if it's a world championship; in that sense, the parallels drawn between her and Eddy Merckx are quite in order. Winning means everything to her, which makes us very different people. I've never been able to match that desire or killer instinct and I have no desire to, either, because I am keen to have a balanced life.

I kept chipping away at the races and ended up with quite a few results: the young rider's jersey in the Tour de l'Aude, which was then one of the biggest stage races on the calendar, and the young rider's jersey in the Giro d'Italia, then as now one of the major events. I had a third attempt at the world road championship, this time in the southern Swiss town of

Mendrisio; Emma had a good chance of winning on a really hard climber's course that suited her, while Nicole had come off the form that she had enjoyed in the past. That meant Great Britain had a bit of a two-pronged leadership, but without any general direction, while my job was similar to the year before; at this stage, it didn't affect me greatly.

The Tour de l'Ardèche was where I earned the contract that moved me several rungs up the ladder. I finished third overall, won the sixth stage and the points rankings, and that led Thomas Campana, the manager of Cervélo, to give me the option to sign with him. Run in tandem with the men's pro team backed by the bike company, rather than the usual commercial backer from outside the sport, Cervélo had enjoyed a massively successful 2009 with riders like Emma Pooley, Kirsten Wild, Claudia Häusler and Kristin Armstrong; signing with them would be a huge step up. While Lotto had staff – I had my first massage there from a team soigneur, for example – none of the riders had a salary they could live off; Cervélo, on the other hand, had a minimum wage across the board. It wasn't a formal meeting with Thomas: at the Ardèche, we were staying in campsites so I had to sneak up to the entrance of one campsite after dark, to meet him in his Cervélo camper, which was all decked out with red stickers. That vehicle alone underlined the contrast; at Lotto, we were still getting changed in the backs of team cars.

Thomas told me that he thought I had potential, and

he offered me a contract and a car. While I was mulling it over, I had a call from the HighRoad team, which was also run in association with a men's team, but with the twist that Bob Stapleton, the team's owner, had run the women's squad before taking over the men's pro team that eventually became Mark Cavendish's HTC. I met their manager Ronny Lauke, but we didn't hit it off and so there was no contract. But I do remember the figure he quoted: 'For a rider like you,' he said, 'we would probably offer 15,000.' I didn't know if he had said 15 or 50 and I didn't dare ask him, but 15 was in the ballpark of what was on the table at Cervélo.

* * *

The Cervélo Test Team training camp in Portugal that winter was an eye-opener. The radical element was that the men's and women's teams were run jointly, and so we were all under the same roof for training camps: the men's team, the sponsors, the journalists. The idea came from Cervélo's founder, Gerard Vroomen, and probably had its roots in the fact that Cervélo had moved across from sponsoring athletes in IronMan, where that kind of gender parity is a given. In other words, they had come from outside the traditional cycling environment and realised there was a market in women's cycling. They gave me proper kit, with my name on it, and a Cervélo bike, which I loved – it seemed to ride itself without any effort on my part – and at one training camp, I met my future husband, Philip Deignan, for the first time.

The only interaction we had – Phil remembers this, I don't – was at the dessert buffet. Apparently we were standing there together; he said, 'I think we had better stay away from here' and I said, 'Yeah' but still got a dessert; he didn't. I just remember him as the Irish guy with the lovely eyes – that is what all the girls said: 'Oh, did you see that Irish guy with the eyes...' Neither of us had any inkling back then of how it would pan out when we met again a few years later, but we do have a team photo with both of us in it.

Phil was one of a strong line-up in the men's team that included Thor Hushovd, the 2008 Tour de France winner Carlos Sastre, and Britons Jeremy Hunt and Dan Lloyd. They weren't the biggest stars in the men's scene, but both teams had phenomenal seasons in 2010, which came down to one unique factor: the environment in Cervélo was absolutely right, with the mix of directors and staff and riders working together perfectly. The women's squad won over 40 races that year, culminating in Emma's world time-trial title that autumn; my personal contribution was five victories, including a stage at the Tour de l'Aude, another at the Route de France and three in a row at the Tour de l'Ardèche.

I didn't make the brightest start to my time at Cervélo: I was involved in the worst crash of my career in my first race in Qatar, which Kirsten Wild was to win overall. I was trying to do my job properly for my new teammates and put my hand up to go to the back of the peloton to get bottles. I waited and waited there for ages at the back of the group with my hand up. I couldn't see any sign of a team car, so I turned around to look for it, but right at that moment I went into a pothole, upended the bike, and landed on the crash barrier. I was in pieces; I woke up on the spinal board in the ambulance with everyone speaking Arabic around me and no idea where I was.

I was taken to hospital with a blanket up to my neck, because all the male doctors weren't allowed to see me; the nurses would come in and scrub my wounds, but I didn't really know what was going on. All you can see when you regain consciousness in that situation is the ceiling above you; it was very disorientating. Eventually someone from the race organisation turned up and I was cleared to leave hospital; they took me to the police station in my shredded Lycra and I was made to sign a waiver, to say that I wouldn't sue the organisation for what had happened. It was immensely intimidating: all these guys looking at a Western woman in not much clothing; I had to trust a bloke who couldn't speak any English to get me back to the race hotel.

It took a long while to get over, but fortunately I had almost two months before the world track championships in Copenhagen. We had found out the previous December about the transformation in the Olympic track programme to create medal parity between men and women: out went the points race, my favourite event, and in came the team pursuit and omnium. That meant my training with Great Britain went over entirely to the team pursuit, which I didn't relish. Team pursuit had a generic coaching programme: all the riders would be given the same training on the track, and as individuals you would have no option but to do the training you were given on any set day.

I didn't agree with that because I believe that even though the team pursuit is a team event, the athletes involved in it are still quite different. For example, your man one – the starter – needs to be a different athlete to get the team up to speed compared to your man four, who needs to have more endurance. From a technical perspective, team pursuiters need to spend the hours together on the boards so that they can build the skills for riding in the wheels, but if you coach each athlete individually then there is more room for improvement. I had tried to discuss this with the GB coaches, but with no obvious result.

Copenhagen was successful, however, with two more medals coming my way: silver in the team pursuit along with Wendy and Jo, and again the omnium, which was five events in a single day, as the UCI were still trying to find the ideal format. There was no elimination – yet – but the scratch and points were made for me, and I gained ground there on the eventual gold medallist, Tara Whitten of Canada. On the other hand, there were three timed disciplines, the flying 200m, 500m time trial, and pursuit, and in all those Tara

97

was well ahead, eventually taking gold, six omnium points in front, while I hung on in the 500m, the last event, to take the silver by a single point.

There were other changes in 2010. I'd traded in the Audi for a Skoda Roomster, which I loved because it had Cervélo stickers all over it – everyone knew that I was a pro – and midway through the season, Adam and I moved into a place of our own a couple of miles away from Tim and Jos. We had been paying Tim and Jos £500 a month, and we had figured we could get somewhere a lot nicer for £600. Moving out was quite a hard thing to do: it involved speaking to Flemish landlords, getting a Belgian bank account, and learning how to recycle the rubbish Belgian-style. The system is that you have lots of different bags, but if the various items aren't in the right one, they don't get taken away by the bin men. It is really good in theory, but we didn't understand it, so we ended up with bags and bags of rubbish piled up at the side of the house. But I loved it: I was living my own life, and it was a huge contrast to being miserable living in Manchester.

* * *

Things were changing among the top women in British Cycling as well. Since her stellar 2008, Nicole Cooke's form hadn't been as good as in the past – it was impossible to say whether she was losing the edge physically, or slipping backwards because the standard was rising among the rest of the riders and making the racing more competitive as a result. Nicole was frustrated by that, and at the same time, Emma was reaching her peak, winning the women's Tour de France and World Cup classics such as Plouay and the Flèche Wallonne.

One sign of that transition came at the national championship in Lancashire in June 2010. At the start of the race, Nicole's dad said in front of the whole peloton that we – the three Cervélo riders, me, Emma and Sharon Laws – were not allowed to work as a team. That is the rule at a national championship, and we did genuinely say to each other we were not going to work as a team in the usual sense. However, we were not going to work against each other either; it was just that we all wanted the opportunity to win. Emma put in a random attack with about 600 metres to go, Nicole couldn't follow any more and Emma won the title; I won the silver. That was great for us, but Nicole refused to go on the podium. In her autobiography, she claimed that Sharon and I had been towed back to her and Emma by our team car when the group split; I can categorically state that this was not the case.

The end of the season was centred on the world championship in Geelong, Australia, and the Commonwealth Games in Delhi. In Geelong, we were working for Emma in the road race – that was the decision in the pre-race meeting – and Nicole made a random attack late on with Judith Arndt to take fourth, which set the cat among the pigeons.

Emma took gold in the time trial, the first time a British woman had managed this, so a huge achievement, and then we went straight to India.

That Commonwealth Games took place against a debate over whether or not British athletes should go due to the venues being incomplete and poor living conditions in the village. I opted to go, and I will always be happy that I did. This was the first multi-sport games I competed in, and remains one of the most pleasant experiences of my career. Arriving at the airport and being greeted by policemen with guns as we got off the plane was a little bit intimidating, but once you actually got to the village, although it was half-finished, the volunteers and other people working there were some of the friendliest people you could ever meet. The road race was somewhat surreal because there were no crowds and everything was fenced off, but the England team – the academy girls, Sharon and Emma – worked well for me in the sprint on the flat course, and I ended up with silver behind Rochelle Gilmore. I had good enough legs to think I could have won it, but I hesitated in the sprint and ended up having to take a less direct line than Rochelle to the finish line.

Cervélo remains a model of how women's and men's professional teams could co-exist, but its days were numbered. The Canadian bike company that had sponsored the Test Team pulled out at the end of the season and the whole set-up was absorbed into the Garmin-Slipstream squad run by Jonathan Vaughters, a former teammate of Lance Armstrong's. The merger just didn't work, at least as far as the women's team was concerned: it involved a very European set-up joining with a very American one. What the change meant was that the women's team now felt like an afterthought. For example, at the training camp, rather than being in the same hotel as the men we were in a separate one. It felt as if the contracts were being honoured as part of the merger deal, but lip service was being paid to what Cervélo had represented and how it had been run.

The contrast was summed up by a weird incident at the one hotel we did share with the men, which was on the night of the team presentation. I got there and went to bed. At about half past 11 there was a knock on the door. It was one of the management, saying, 'You need to come downstairs – there is a party for one of the male riders. My reaction was: 'Fine. Why? OK.'

I went down to the bar and discovered that I was the only girl in the room. I was left with no choice but to take part in a dance competition with the birthday boy in front of everybody, with all the other male riders sitting on bar stools in a line watching the two of us. It was a sort of Wii game where you follow the moves on a computer screen and you have to stand on the mat with your feet at the right spots; that was it, and then I was allowed to go to bed.

I felt like a complete fool and I remember trying to work out exactly what was going on. I kept asking myself, 'Why did that happen?' I felt desperately confused: should I be flattered because I was the only woman invited? Were they taking the piss out of me? I was naïve; only later did I realise that they were not showing me the respect I deserved. I was not being seen or treated as a colleague with equal standing. I was being used as entertainment. I was trivialised.

CHAPTER 6

END OF
THE TRACK

On training days, the Manchester velodrome felt like a hospital or a public swimming bath: a sterile environment, with no colour on the walls, lino on the floors, long corridors with no windows and the velodrome aroma. For a World Cup, Manchester was a great venue, but without music, crowds and a full-house atmosphere it was cold and bleak. When I walked out through the airlock swing doors on 1 October 2011 it was the best feeling I could remember in years. I felt my shoulders lighten amid a huge sense of relief that I wouldn't be returning for a long time.

A year earlier, in September 2010, I'd still had every intention of continuing as a track cyclist as well as a road racer. My plan for the 20 months leading up to the London

Olympic Games was to target both the omnium on the track – which would involve doing the team pursuit as well – and the road race. There was a problem, however: at that point – before the rise of Laura Trott – I was the only Great Britain woman who was interested in riding the omnium and there was no particular enthusiasm for the discipline among the coaching staff. British Cycling were focused on the team pursuit, which was a timed event, and a more secure bet for a medal. Bunched races on the track – points, scratch, Madison – had always been seen as an afterthought, ridden by team pursuiters when they had completed the main business. That left me with one option: I would have to be my own trainer and work it out for myself.

My self-coaching system would become more sophisticated and specific over time, but in the beginning I found it complex and stressful. The omnium format had been stabilised at six events: flying lap, scratch race, 3,000m pursuit, elimination (sometimes called 'devil take the hindmost'), points race and 500m time trial. That was complicated in itself, but because of the mix of disciplines and my ambitions on the road, I felt if I wanted to go for the omnium place in London: I was going to devise my own programme.

Fortunately, I had some help from Westy; endurance racing on the track was his domain, so he knew what it involved. By this point, however, I had left the Great Britain academy, because I no longer qualified as an under-23. That meant there was no accommodation for me in Manchester and I was no longer supported to live there, although my medals in the world track championship meant I was still a funded rider. Jo had bought a house – she was always clever and sensible and seemed to have a bit of cash – so I moved in temporarily with Westy, Cara and their son; I would stay with them during the week and go home to Otley most weekends. Living with Westy and Cara felt like a home from home but there is no substitute for having your own space.

At this time Paul Manning took over from Dan Hunt as women's endurance coach. I found adjusting to working with Paul difficult. As an athlete you constantly feel under pressure to be ready for the next competition and as a result it's very rare to have a period of time where you feel comfortable making major changes. Paul and I just didn't click. I wasn't completely confident in his ability to coach me any better than I could coach myself; after all, I had won more international points races than he had. Forming trusting relationships takes time and commitment on both sides and I don't think Paul or I really gave it a chance. At the same time, there was expectation for the road from Garmin-Cérvelo. The management there had changed as well: the logistics manager, Theo Marther, had taken over; to begin with he was looking for a coach or directeur sportif to support him, but he couldn't find one, so he decided to take on the role himself, but ultimately he wasn't really suited to the job.

These external pressures all meant I was struggling at the

start of 2011, what with trying to figure out how to balance the six events of the omnium and attempting to build up for the road season, all with a lack of support from anyone within British Cycling. The problem was that you have to be both a sprinter and able to perform in a 20-kilometre points race. I tried identifying my weaknesses – which were in the timed events – and focusing on those events rather than the bunched races. I picked the brains of the sprint coach Iain Dyer about standing starts and flying laps and spoke to Jo about the individual pursuit; she helped me work out the training sessions.

However, I was spread too thin; I became tired and stressed, and developed stomach problems. I would go to training sessions and end up keeled over in agony in a corner. With about two weeks to go to the world track championships, which were to be held in the Netherlands that March, I was diagnosed as having a stomach ulcer; rather than the medical team pulling me out, I had to make the decision for myself. Athletes can be very bad at making the correct decisions when it comes to their own health, so I believe that the medical team should always have the confidence to make those calls.

I went home, recovered and slept on the sofa for weeks before I got myself back together. By then, Jo had been to Apeldoorn, and had become world team-pursuit champion again; she and Dan then arranged a holiday in Lanzarote. I knew that I needed to get fit for the road season and, to do that, I would have to put in a lot of miles, and I couldn't stay in England to get those miles in. I opted for Lanzarote because, since Jo and Dan were going, there would be at least a couple of people I knew on the island if I needed anything. So I set up my own training camp: I rented my own place, a little apartment in the old town, and cooked for myself for two weeks. I saw Dan and Jo for a pizza one night and that was all. It was brutal: Lanzarote is windy, flat and boring, all of which made my time there character building and a decent foundation for a good season on the road.

That year, 2011, I started to feel confident in finish sprints. I won fewer races overall, but the quality was higher. The key moment came at the Tour of Chongming Island, a three-day stage race held in May near Shanghai, where I took a major scalp to win stage 1: Ina-Yoko Teutenberg of Germany. Riding for HTC-Colombia, Teutenberg had been a prolific sprinter since the early 2000s and was still the best in the world. It felt like a massive breakthrough, and although I didn't manage to get the better of her again that week, I finished just behind her in the Chongming World Cup race that comes a couple of days later. Sprint finishes are the natural thing to target when you move from the track to the road, because of the leg speed, race sense and bike handling you bring from the track, but this marked the beginning of another transition: when you are young, you can win sprints in easier races if you are fast, but you don't have the strength to get to the end of a harder event in any shape to sprint. Gradually, I was acquiring that strength. And after Chongming, I had no doubt: the world road championships that autumn would be on a flattish course in Copenhagen, I'll make it a target.

I travelled to Denmark with a fair degree of confidence. I'd had a strong summer, starting by outsprinting Nicole Cooke to win the national championship in Northumberland by several lengths. The two of us had broken away early on a tough course with my Garmin teammates, Emma Pooley and Sharon Laws, and then the equation was relatively simple: I knew I was the fastest sprinter so I would have the best chance in the finish and I had only to bide my time – 'to be lazy', as I said afterwards. I followed that with a stage win and the points title at the Thüringen Rundfahrt – again getting close to Teutenberg in a sprint, and riding strongly out of breakaways – and I did so wearing the national champion's jersey, which was sweet after two silver medals in a row.

There was a different atmosphere among the British team in Copenhagen. Usually the world road-race championships felt relatively low-key compared to the track; they had seemed like a bit of a poor relation because of British Cycling's focus on Olympic track medals, but this resembled a track Worlds in terms of the amount of staff, the riders who were there, and the media attention. As far as team support went, it was the best Worlds I have ever attended:

there was a chef in attendance, and even an introductory meeting for all the riders at the start of the week. We had always had a good chance at the road Worlds with Nicole, pretty much every year since 2003. The difference here was that after struggling for years, the men had a strong shout thanks to Mark Cavendish, hence the entourage.

We had a good look at the course during the week and it was clear it was going to be a sprint finish: it was flat, with barely a hill on the mainly urban course. We sat down together with a whiteboard – all the girls, Shane Sutton and Simon Cope – to plan the race, but one thing was clear: I was the favourite because I could sprint; I was the one the team was going to work for, and with a team of seven, as big as we'd ever qualified for a world road-race championship, we would have a decent chance. Nicole had had a poor. To be fair to her, at this point in the meeting she did speak up and say she was not happy about my being the leader, and that she should be able to have a chance as well. She'd said her piece, and that was the meeting over.

Getting into the back end of the race, there were six of us – Emma, Sharon, Lucy Martin, Katie Colclough and Catherine Hare – working as a team; I could see everybody apart from Nicole. With about 900 metres to go, just before the last corner where the road began dragging upwards towards the finish, there was a crash in front of me; a Canadian girl fell and her bike went right across the road. I was caught behind and had to stop behind her. I didn't have to unclip from the pedals, but I had to come to a dead stand and find my way round her, then accelerate back to full speed again on that uphill road, with no momentum to help me.

This was the moment where Nicole should have been looking out for me; she had been told that morning that she was to lead me out, but she had gone into that last corner in fourth position, on Marianne Vos's wheel; that was the position where she eventually finished in the sprint. She should have been there to pull me to the final metres; instead I had to do it all myself, but I still managed to find the speed and momentum to end up seventh in spite of coming from a standstill and finding my way through the traffic with no teammate to help me. Bearing in mind how fast the other riders would have been travelling in that final kilometre, if I could get back in the mix in that way, I have to say I had a real chance at a medal. A real chance. It was one of those rare days when you feel like you are floating.

Immediately afterwards I rode back down the finish straight to the pits, went into the GB team cabin, put my head in my hands and wept. My first thought was, 'How could she do that?' I let the people around me know how disappointed I was, and after that I was ushered away and went back to the hotel. That is one of only two times I have ever cried in cycling, both of them in instances when I have been let down by teammates and have been left in a state of shock. I think when that happens the anger is less about the disappointment of not winning, more about the fact that the work you put in previously hasn't been recognised. That might not affect me now, but as a naïve young rider you have the idea that you will get back what you put in. The only other time I have had a similar reaction was in the Giro in 2012: I had been working tirelessly for Shelley Olds all year – I thought we had a relationship and she was meant to help me and lead me out – but she didn't.

We had a meeting that evening, to debrief after what had happened. Nicole's explanation was that she had been looking for me and she couldn't see me, so she went for the finish herself. To some extent, I can now see it from her point of view: she had had a poor year and given how driven she is, it was not surprising that she thought she had a chance for herself. She didn't understand that she wasn't fast enough; she had never really been a pure sprinter. However, if I think about the position I am in now, if, in three years' time, Lucy Garner has a similar opportunity – which potentially could happen as Lucy has that talent and she is a fine sprinter – and I am at a point in my career where I am coming off my peak, then I would like to think that I would help her. That's sport, isn't it? That's professionalism. Nicole didn't have that mirror in which to look at herself; she still just wanted success so badly.

What happened in Copenhagen doesn't hurt any more, however. Part of the pain I felt at the time was because I was an underdog; I was still finding my way up the ladder. If something like this were to happen now, and I really felt like

I had lost the world title because of it, I would do something about it. However, I will never get total closure on that episode because Nicole would never work for me. She never helped me out in a race, which means she never recognised me for what I am.

In the background to the issue with Nicole at Copenhagen in 2011 was a bigger picture. The British Cycling system was not set up in a way that encouraged the women road racers to work together. This was in glaring contrast with the long-term approach that was taken by Rod Ellingworth to winning Mark Cavendish's world title in 2011 on that same Copenhagen course. There was very little to foster team spirit. If Marianne Vos wins a world championship medal, all the Dutch team who have contributed to that medal receive funding as a result. The difference is that British riders are relying on funding from British Cycling – in this case a placing in the top eight secures your funding – but if you are part of the team that achieved a result you don't get anything. For the Italians or the Dutch, if you are on the road team you get the funding from the medal, equal funding for the whole team. In the British system there is nothing, no recognition. One of the things that Rod Ellingworth did was to ensure that all the men would share in any success by any one of their number.

It's an odd one. There is an expectation of professionalism that I agree with but on the other hand, why would you sacrifice your chance for another girl just because she is

British? You haven't raced with her as a teammate all season because you only come together as a team for the road Worlds. You haven't had a chance to get to know her. When you put that together with the economic instability in women's racing, where teams aren't secure and contracts are small or non-existent for most of the riders, you could almost say that with individual funding on the line there is a disincentive to work as a team and sacrifice yourself for your teammates.

The lack of consistent management of the women's squad within British Cycling and the lack of support also had a part to play in what happened in Copenhagen. We didn't have any team training camps. The Dutch go to South Africa for two weeks every single year and they go to Gran Canaria as a national team every February, with the option of two camps there in January and February. Plus they also have an altitude training camp in May. We still don't have that or anything like it.

One of British Cycling's biggest failings is that they have never put someone in place to work for the women road cyclists over the long term in the way that Rod clearly did for the men, and that is still the case five years on. Although Simon Cope would fight for little bits and pieces here and there, there has not been one single character within the organisation looking after women road cyclists or fighting our corner. It's always been 'whoever has got half a job takes it on', which means that as a woman cyclist you never had a clear idea of what you were signing up for when you rode for British Cycling. After the Halfords sponsorship ended and once Beijing was out of the way, the support level dropped, although I never delved into why.

I understand to some extent. Shane Sutton told me that he didn't feel there was a full-time job for someone to run the women's road programme, but that was because British Cycling didn't have the cross-over that there was with the under-23 men's programme; that changed in 2016 when the women's academy was started up again. Before that, if a young rider like Anna Christian wanted to be a road racer she had no avenue within British Cycling, whereas a young man of comparable age and talent had the option of getting on to the under-23 academy. That said, I would never put any weight behind a rider giving British Cycling's lack of support as a reason for a failed career; you need to want it so much more than that.

*   *   *

It had been a while since I began to become aware that I actively disliked the track. It was what you could call a love–hate relationship: I loved the bunched events, the scratch and points, and the track was where I had begun. Luck plays a part in the scratch, but points racing is something I will always love. I would dearly like to be world champion in the discipline before I retire. Few things are better than dictating how a points race happens; the other riders are like your puppets, and you can ride rings round them. It's painful, but you are in control; there is a fabulous feeling when you get the rush on someone just in time to snatch the five points from them for winning a sprint. And the suffering is like nothing else; the last 20 laps can seem eternal.

The problems lay within the system I had to work with in order to ride the track. During 2010 I couldn't help making the comparison between British Cycling and Cervélo. With my road team, I had felt as if I was taken seriously, treated as a professional, like an athlete. At British Cycling I felt as if I was just a cog in a system. I didn't feel like a valued member of a team. I felt trust from my road team, whereas on the track it was a bit different. As long as you were performing you were fine, but when you were not, then things changed. It seemed as if you were disposable.

I didn't like the lack of personal control. I wasn't happy with the teacher–student relationship I had with the people there and I wasn't one for the politics of it, the frictions between the different tiers within the coaching staff. There just didn't seem to be respect between the coaching staff; it was as if everybody was ducking and diving and having to watch their own back. It didn't feel like a team to me. What's more, I began to realise it had always felt like that.

It was a more limited world. The track involved spending so much time in Manchester, always with the same people. Day to day when I was on the track I was constantly analysed. Every single thing I did was recorded. There was no chance of simply riding your bike for enjoyment. I could sense from rubbing shoulders with Beijing gold medallists like Vicky Pendleton and Rebecca Romero that they had clearly been unhappy on the way to winning their medals, and it also seemed that once they had actually won them, that didn't change their lives in the way they had expected. None of this struck me overnight; the feeling grew on me in the years after I struck out on my own and began to forge a career for myself. Essentially, I grew up.

After Copenhagen, the next item on the agenda was the national track championships in the Manchester velodrome. I was determined to prove my ability on the track, in spite of having pulled out of that year's world championships, trying to coach myself and being told I wasn't a good track rider. I thought, 'Right, I will go back to the track nationals' – where the track squad would be racing – 'and I will show you who is the best points rider and scratch race rider despite having no support or track training.' I smashed it and won gold in the points and scratch, I said thanks, and walked out through that door. From now on, I had decided, I would be fully focused on the road.

I was proud: I had wanted to stamp my authority on those races to prove I was the best in Britain. I didn't feel I had been given the opportunity to be the country's best omnium rider. I was anxious, but in my guts I knew it was the right decision. There was trepidation about what the next chapter would be, but no doubt in my mind. I felt as if a weight had physically been lifted off my shoulders: I felt taller and lighter, as if I was walking out of a cloud. I felt as though I had been completely set free.

* * *

I had driven round the London Olympic road race course during the men's test event with Simon Cope in a Great Britain team car – there was no test race for women, as would be the case going into Rio four years later – which made it clear that the home Olympics would suit me: a flat finish on the Mall coming after a hilly middle section where we could get rid of the pure sprinters. Publicly I had buried the hatchet with Nicole but the obvious question of how Great Britain would gel as a team was hanging in the air.

There were two main outcomes from the problems we'd had in Copenhagen. Simon Cope left; his successor was to be Chris Newton, a former team pursuiter who was to combine the job of running the under-23 men's academy with looking after the women's road team during the build-up to London. The other was that I did an interview with *Cycle Sport* magazine in which I set out the facts about Copenhagen. It was a classic case of being young and naïve and not knowing what I was letting myself in for; Copenhagen was a small part of the interview but it turned into the whole of it. I had to stand by what I said, but relations between Nicole and me became the story of the British women's team going into London; generally that was what the mainstream media picked upon to write about. I was asked about it constantly.

The autumn of 2011 was fraught: Adam and I split up again, something we seemed to do at most opportunities. That meant I was homeless for a while, and wondering where to live. Meanwhile, Adam moved from Belgium to Monaco, and so when we got back together in December I moved down there midway through the month. With that settled, the question of which team I would ride for in the build-up to London was suddenly and unexpectedly thrown at me. I was at a Great Britain training camp in Majorca on 22 December when I got confirmation that my contract with Garmin-Cervélo was not going to be honoured for 2012.

Going into Olympic year, with the road now my focus, this was a nightmare. By December every team has filled its roster for the coming year, so you can't say to people, 'Make room for me in your team, please.' Plus, it's not far off the beginning of the next season, so the key people who make the decision are already on their training camps with their teams. There had been instability in the past, but that year was the scariest time I have known, because my track funding from British Cycling had gone as well, and on the road I had gone down to basic funding. Financially, that was manageable, just about, but it was going to be difficult. It was very unnerving. I barely slept at that training camp.

It didn't help that the way Garmin handled the break-up of

the team was just appalling. I phoned their contract people initially but couldn't get through to anybody, so then we had a crisis Skype call between all the riders in the women's team and the team manager Theo Maucher, who was on our side and wanted to help us out. The question was simple: do we stick together as a team and try and find a sponsor, or do we go our separate ways? As often happens in this situation, initially there was a commitment that we would try to stay together, but then one by one you would hear that somebody had signed here, somebody else had signed there, and eventually you realised you would have no choice but to look after yourself. Then it was a matter of waiting minute by minute for something to happen.

That is where my dad came into his own; he has a lot of knowledge of employment law, because that is one of his specialities. He was great when it came to looking through my contracts and sending the right emails to Jonathan Vaughters, who was trying to put me into a corner by claiming that I had looked elsewhere before my contract was ended. That was what they had been trying to do: put off telling us that the team was folding so that people would abandon ship right up until they had made that call, thereby relieving them of any responsibility.

The Great Britain training camp where I heard the news from Garmin was in Majorca, in Alcudia – combined with Team Sky – so I sat down in the restaurant with Dave Brailsford, who had heard what was going on. He actually tried to contact Vaughters himself and couldn't get through. Dave said that British Cycling could put a national team programme together, but I didn't want that, even though obviously it was a sign that they recognised what I was capable of and they certainly didn't want to see me left high and dry. My thinking was that I didn't want to walk away from all the control I had been able to gain, and then go straight back into something I had left. I wasn't going to get paid. I was to be what amounted to a GB number plate, supporting their track programme on the road. That wasn't really a viable option.

Enter Danny Stam. I had begun negotiating with the Skil-Shimano team – later to become Liv-Plantur – but Cervélo came up with a package deal. They were still sponsoring Garmin, and they have always been huge supporters of women's racing, so they wanted to rescue the riders that were out of contract. Cervélo approached the Dutch team AA Drinks, who had been around since 2005, and offered to supply them with bikes if they took on the group of Garmin riders who had been left high and dry. When I had an email from Danny asking for a meeting, my first response was, 'Thanks for the interest but I'm actually in negotiations with someone else, so I am not able to talk.' Then he called: 'I know what kind of rider you are,' he said, and he listed all my results. Clearly, he had done his research. That made me think perhaps he knew what he was talking about, so I signed up from there.

The deal with AA Drinks was finalised on New Year's Day 2012. I had come from two squads that were part of men's teams, so this one would be smaller, a total of 15 riders. Four British women had come across from Garmin – me, Emma, Sharon and Lucy Martin, plus Carla Ryan and Jessie Daems. The main sponsor was a sports drink, with backing from the former Dutch world champion Leontien Van Moorsel; her husband Michel Zijlaard was the general manager, and the strongest riders were Shelley Olds of America, and Holland's Kirsten Wild.

When I had been riding for British Cycling's track programme in my academy days, Adam and Pete Kennaugh used to wear really high socks, right up their calves, when they were doing Madison training, and talk about Slippens and Stam. I didn't know who they were talking about but I remembered the names and put two and two together when I met them: Robert Slippens was Danny's regular six-day partner. Danny had been riding for AA Drink on the track where they were his private sponsor, and then he moved into the management of the women's team; he had only just retired, so that was his transition into civilian life. He was still in good shape so he would come on training rides with us, which was another thing I really liked about him; he still does that now. I think it's really valuable.

Danny has a fair few stories; clearly he had a lot of fun when he was a rider. He's a bit of a ducker and diver; for example, when you ask him, 'Why did you decide to retire?'

he says, 'Well, when I paid off my house I had this much money in the bank; that is when I stopped riding the six days because I could retire mortgage free.' He was always making deals and surviving, but in an honest way.

The Dutch are famous for being very direct but early on you could tell it was Danny's first time working with a women's team. He wouldn't sugar coat things. If you were fat he would say you were fat and if you needed to train harder he would say that you needed to train harder. There was no attempt to be tactful and that didn't work out with a few of the girls. My view was that he was a professional and we were getting paid to do a job, so we should be told if we were too fat.

In a way, every cloud had a silver lining, this one being that the demise of Garmin threw me together with Danny. We had actually ridden the Amsterdam Six Day at the same time at the end of 2008 when he was competing at the end of his career with Slippens. They were Netherland's most celebrated six-day pairing of the time, a classic combination of sprinter and stayer, and Danny was the engine of the partnership, the engine and the brains, while Slippens was the sprinter.

Our partnership was to be key in my career as well. I handled his directness a lot better than some of the other riders, but the main reason we get on so well is that, like me, Danny achieves balance in his life. We click, and over the years our relationship has developed into a kind of friendship; he has a similar mindset to me, with his family being more important than cycling. Together with Phil West, Danny is the only coach I have learnt to trust over the years. If you are in Danny's circle of friends, then you can rely on him for anything.

CHAPTER 7

2012

When I was a kid, my uncle Andy always took me to rugby practice to play alongside my cousin Edward, who is my age and a big bruiser of a lad and who eventually played for England. Uncle Andy had gone to the same school in Otley as my parents and my auntie Anne – my father's sister – and was a classic good-looking athletic guy, who would do practice every lunchtime and had new Adidas rugby boots before anyone else. Andy started out as an architect, then became a primary school teacher, and still lived in Otley with auntie Anne, Edward and my other cousin, Alistair.

The first hint that something was not quite right came during Christmas 2011. On Christmas Day our immediate family were to get together, Boxing Day was all the

Armitsteads, the day after Boxing Day, my mum's side of the family – we always do it this way. On Boxing Day that year everyone was supposed to come to our house. Uncle Andy wasn't there, which was kind of strange.

A couple of months later, on 4 March 2012, I won the race at Tielt-Winge, the Omloop van het Hageland, just up the road from my old home at Tim and Jos's. I was in Brussels airport on my own about to fly back to Monaco when the phone rang; it was Dad.

What he had to tell me was heartbreaking. Uncle Andy had hung himself. I called my cousin Edward straight away and his reaction was, 'Thank you for calling, because people are often too scared to.' It turned out that uncle Andy had only been depressed from Christmas onwards. We had had no idea of this, so it was a massive shock to all of us.

I just wanted to get home. That was the most important thing. I got myself back to Yorkshire and we had a family funeral. There was such a sense of waste and loss. I had never experienced a death so close to home before; it was a difficult time for my whole family. Uncle Andy came hand in hand with sport throughout my childhood, he always had enthusiasm for competition and fun, we shared similar passions for sport. My relationship with Edward became considerably stronger; cycling and the worries surrounding the Olympics during this time became completely irrelevant.

Everything seemed to be happening at the same time. It wasn't long afterwards that I had a call from my friend

Az's brother to say Az had had a bad lupus episode, and they didn't know how it was going to turn out; he had only been given a 50-50 chance of getting through it. That was another awful, brutal blow. I sent Az about 100 messages; I went to visit him in hospital quite a few times. Gradually he got better and after that the rest of my friends – that close-knit group I described earlier – decided to cycle from Leeds to London to the Olympics in aid of a lupus charity. That was something positive that came out of it and Az was able to join them on a couple of the stops, which was lovely.

Uncle Andy's suicide changed everyone in my family; it was a big shake-up for the very strong, close-knit group that we had thought we were. It gave us perspective, it made us closer, and we became more prepared to talk about our emotions. Generally, we are not like that at all; we are probably still not good enough at expressing our feelings, but now we take each other's worries more seriously. It was a life-changing moment for me. I had never experienced a death so close to me and it made me admire how strong other people could be whilst grieving. I had always had the idea in my mind that if I am upset or down, then going out, going for a walk in the mountains, seeing a beautiful view – that kind of thing – can have a restorative effect. But you have to realise it might not necessarily be that simple, and it might not be like that for everyone.

* * *

In the midst of all this, cycling became a release. When I have challenges in my life, when I am not happy, I find it easier when I am out on my bike. This was one of those periods, as were the various times I had split up with Adam. You go fast on two wheels; you can keep going for hours. You work things out. Cycling is something that you can always control.

On the road, when it came to racing I found my feet. For the first time in my career, unencumbered by the track, I did a proper winter's training, putting in a complete few months of riding in the off-season. I had a proper holiday at the end of 2011 and then I built up in the way that a road rider would, rather than transferring straight into the winter track programme. The difference was immense. As a track rider I might have done one midweek ride and then a long day at the weekend; this winter I began doing what I do now: three-day blocks of riding, and all good hours. I would put in about 20 hours a week; a lot of the time I would be training with Adam and the Belgian Classic specialist Philippe Gilbert, hanging on their coat-tails.

The extra work paid dividends. I was physically stronger than I had ever been, and amid the emotional roller-coaster of that spring I landed two good wins: Hageland – a race with particular significance now, as I always associate it with uncle Andy – was a sprint finish from a three-rider break, with Pauline Ferrand-Prévot of France and Elisa Longo Borghini in my wake. Three weeks later came the first ever women's Gent–Wevelgem and a solo victory in my national champion's jersey after a 40km lone break at the end of the 113 kilometres. The team's plan was simple: I would press on over the climbs, with my teammate Kirsten Wild ready for the sprint if I was caught; my attack on the second ascent, the Baneberg, was speculative, but only one rider, Liesbet de Vocht, came with me. She didn't last long, and with Kirsten and another teammate, Jessie Daems, controlling a chasing group of only five riders, I was never seen again. On a course similar to London – a hilly middle section, a flat run-in to the finish – it was a huge confidence boost.

The reality of the build-up to the Olympic Games hit me one day in spring 2012 when I was walking down Oxford Street. A message came in on my phone, and once I'd read it I looked up to cross the road to go to the Adidas store, and there was a huge photograph of me on the shop front. I had almost walked past it. I thought, 'Whoa, this is a bit crazy.' I had been an Adidas-sponsored athlete since 2009, but had never been used in any advertising campaigns; when I walked into the shop that day there was a huge image of me on my bike and that felt pretty cool. A couple of months later we had the kitting out for the Olympic team, the day after the national championships in Yorkshire – that was like a kid's dream, really, really good fun.

I went through the entire build-up to London working from training programmes I had devised myself, with the Giro d'Italia as the main preparation race. The Giro was awful, however. I developed a urinary infection and diarrhoea, probably as a result of the heat. Chris Newton – bronze medallist in the points in Beijing and the men's under-23 academy manager – had suggested that I continue, because sometimes racing on empty can work as a kind of overload training. Fortunately Danny was there and was having none of it – 'No, you've got to give in and go home to rest' – so I pulled out after six stages. It was a tough journey to Monaco from Milan; the train was like an oven, and I sat in the back carriage next to the toilet, for obvious reasons. It was tough: three weeks out from the Games, I was on my knees, thinking, 'How am I going to handle this?'

Initially I tried to persist with training, but that clearly wasn't working, so I was forced to have four days off. I picked up the training again and went out on my bike with Adam. I remember one ride vividly; it was the week before my last race prior to London, the Thüringen Rundfahrt, and I was riding along, thinking, 'I am still so rubbish. I am so rubbish.'

It was Adam who said to me, 'Lizzie, you are going flat out.'

'Oh.'

'We are full-on here, you are not rubbish.'

Because you are so isolated in that environment – the pre-Olympic pressure cooker – you are capable of telling yourself all sorts of things that aren't true. After that, I didn't train with a power meter. I just went on feel, didn't overanalyse anything, went right back to basics and didn't do too much going into Thüringen; I raced well there and that was me set fair for the Olympics.

British Cycling's input in the run-in had been limited. I had had a phone call with Shane Sutton about team selection – who they were thinking of, and what did I think – and that was that. I had a race suit fitting, and had been given my flight details, and had been told that Chris Newton would be running the team. There was no programme for us and I had never worked with Chris before. He had shown his face at the Giro; one of the girls from AA Drinks said to me at the airport, 'Your coach is really good-looking', and my reaction was, 'Who can she be talking about?' Then I saw Chris across the concourse and thought, 'Oh, that's who she means.'

I knew that the sprint would be important in London, so I was determined to have electric gears. I had to buy them myself. I also remember being really frustrated because I did not find out that I was doing the time trial until I had caught the plane to London, so I didn't have a time-trial bike with me. I had assumed the time triallists would be Nicole and Emma, but Lucy Martin told me on the flight to London that she had seen on the Internet that it would be me and Emma. I called Danny, because I knew that our team mechanic would be coming over as we had a lot of Olympic riders in AA Drinks. The mechanic had several bikes, so I asked Danny if there was anyone else's time-trial bike in there that

I could use. They had one that fitted, which belonged to one of the Russians, so I went round the hotel grounds on it, and said, 'Well, that will do', and I didn't worry a lot after that; I had to focus on the road race, so I just went down to the Great Britain team hotel at Foxhills in Surrey, determined to get on with the job.

After I arrived there, Chris Newton suggested a three-hour motor-pacing session, which was totally different to the training that I had planned for myself. He wasn't trying to sabotage me, he just saw things differently. If I'd not been the strong-willed character that I am, I'd have ended up doing the final days differently from the way I'd planned them. Westy and Danny said I should just stick to the programme I'd set for myself.

The atmosphere in Foxhills was bizarre, because Bradley Wiggins had just won the Tour de France, with Mark Cavendish and Chris Froome in support. You would come down to breakfast and there would be Bradley sitting there reading a paper with a big picture of himself all over the front page. In that situation, you think: 'What do I say here?' and there is only one thing: 'Congratulations!' You have to say it even though you are aware that you are one of a million people saying it. He says, 'Oh, cheers girls.' They had all come from the Tour, so they had their wives and girlfriends with them for the first couple of days.

The food was made for us all by the Team Sky chef; nowadays it would sit well with me, being very vegetable-heavy, but back then my diet was very different and his recipes left my stomach in pieces. I was thinking, 'I need plain pasta. If I have another vegetable juice I will be sitting on the toilet before the race starts.' One night there was no dessert. It was all fruit, so I said to the waiter, 'Please may I see the dessert menu?'

'We are not allowed to give you menus.'

As for what I answered, we should just say that the stubborn side of me came out and I got my dessert – chocolate-based, I can definitely recall – and it drew a few looks, from the other riders as well as the management.

The day before the road race we watched the men's race on television in the hotel at Foxhills, then headed for the cars to move into the team hotel in Central London, to be handy for the start on the Mall. On the bed there were welcome packs from Team GB, little bits of things like Nivea sun cream with Team GB written on it, a little teddy bear, a bar of chocolate, a little wash bag and so on. I gave it away to family and friends, as I always do. I'm not much of a hoarder; I tend to get rid of stuff quickly, although I do have a memory box at home in which I keep important things. There are only so many tracksuits you can hang on to.

* * *

I looked out of my hotel window on race morning and saw the gold BMWs parked up in the middle of Central London.

It was raining, and that made me smile. I had grown up in that weather. I felt as if it was my terrain. I felt at home in it technically – I would be able to trust my ability going down descents or going for gaps. The Italians and others would have come from fast roads racing in sunshine; I knew that the course would be gritty British lanes that would make a lot of the opposition think they had double punctures. If I could get in a break, organising a chase in the wet would be much harder for the opposition.

We'd had team meetings, which were interesting. The plan boiled down to Emma and Lucy riding for me while Nicole would ride her own race. I was prepared for that; I wasn't bothered. It wasn't because of what had happened in Copenhagen; Nicole just wanted to ride for herself rather than for me. You can't make a character like Nicole ride for someone else if she isn't up for it. It was far better to have all the cards on the table. So the plan was that Lucy would look after me until we got to Box Hill, and then Emma would attack, to start splitting up the race to drop some of the pure sprinters. On the day that worked perfectly.

What I was thinking about was getting in the top ten. I knew it was going to be quite a tactical race, so I didn't want to think too deeply about what might happen. I race better on instinct than with a fixed plan. When I had been a points race rider I had tried having coaches suggest moves from trackside, but I decided that wasn't for me. I race better when I am allowed to do what I feel is right in a given moment.

I was thinking about the race, about riding the race, about how I could get the best out of it.

I wasn't worried about Marianne Vos, even though she was the out and out favourite and I'd never beaten her. Up until 2012 she had been dominant for half a dozen seasons, but this was the first year she had shown a little weakness: she had a month out with a broken collarbone and there were cracks in her form, particularly her sprint. She had been beaten a couple of times in stages at the Giro, although she had still dominated it overall.

It was raining on the start line and the roads were wet all the way through; we were soaking. It ended up being a race like I had never known before. I didn't feel pain in my legs once. It was like a strange out-of-body experience, because normally you'd be thinking, 'How many kilometres to go?' but instead it seemed to pass in a flash. We had two laps of the Box Hill circuit to cover before we headed back into Central London. Marianne attacked on the second climb, on the straight bit just before the road zig-zags. As she went I was stuck on the inside of Clara Hughes, the Canadian. I saw Marianne go and no one went after her – clearly they couldn't – and I must have been on a flyer because I had time to think, 'Why aren't they following?' They simply couldn't. I was blocked in, but I was able to get out and catch her, which is a sign of how good my form was that day.

I sat on Marianne's wheel and thought, 'No, this isn't right, we can't go at this stage, it is too far with just us two.'

So I waited. Over the top, Emma attacked; there were a few more attacks, which meant the field was strung out going into the next little climb, which is Mill Lane. We hit that, and the Russian Olga Zabelinskaya took off; Marianne, Shelley Olds and me went across to her, and I thought, 'Head down, keep going, keep going.' We got to the bottom just before you come to the main roads that take you back into London; I looked behind and we had about 100 metres. Just then it really started to pour down, which was good for us, as it's so hard for a bunch to get organised in the rain. Marianne just went, so I did what she did; Shelley Olds sat on our wheels, which hampered us a bit at first, but about ten kilometres later she punctured. Once she had disappeared there were three of us all going for a medal, so we were all full-on. In that situation you just commit completely and make it work.

I lost my sunglasses in Richmond Park on the way back; luckily enough I had watched the men's race where Fabian Cancellara had fallen on the sharp corner there, so I went gingerly around that one because it was so slippery. I wish the glasses could have recorded what was flashing past them before they fell off; just the crowds – even in the pouring rain there was not a bit of fence with a single space on it for the final ten kilometres. I was totally in the zone, focused, committed, but as we came through the park, my mind drifted off just a little, to my uncle Andy. That was strange. I am not a believer in ghosts or the supernatural, but I did think about him.

I kept my concentration until the last corner on to the Mall, and what happened next is my only regret from that day. Just then, a thought from outside came into my mind: my friends are stood on that corner. I wish I had not thought that, because that was the first time in the race where I had been drawn out of my bubble and into the crowd. With three kilometres to go, I had been thinking about what Westy would tell me: he would want me to sit on. I was consciously thinking like that all the way; I was completely focused on the race until I thought of them standing at that corner. The only might-have-been I have is that there was one moment with about 250 metres to go where Marianne was on the left, Olga was in the middle and I was on the fence in third wheel. There was a small gap between Olga and the fence and I should have gone for it right then; I wish I had jumped because I would have given myself a better shot. I would have caught Marianne napping, but as I got out of the saddle, I hesitated and she went. As it turned out, she was faster in the sprint for the line so I can't regret it. I would just have run her closer. There was a bit of inexperience there. I was happy with a podium place, but you have about a second to make that decision, which is where your racing instincts have to kick in.

The first thing I thought initially when I won the silver medal was just wow. Wow, wow, wow, wow, wow! I remember thinking distinctly about Rio: 'I will get gold next time'. Then I kicked myself and thought, 'You have just got a medal, enjoy this for a second.'

What came afterwards was surreal. As soon as you get

a medal, you are very much owned by the Olympics. The photo I have of the podium looks incredible: you have got the crowds, Buckingham Palace behind you, as you stand there with the medal. But my view was not the greatest: mainly, what I could see were the soldiers who were working for the organisers. There was a small grandstand in front of me, but most of the atmosphere was actually behind me. The podium is all set up for television and photographs; all my family were standing behind me. What was disappointing for me was that I didn't get to embrace any of them. I couldn't find them afterwards and I wasn't allowed to go looking; the soldiers wouldn't let me. I was thinking, 'Let me out, let me out', but they didn't.

For 24 hours after you win a medal you are the property of the British Olympic Association, so you have to do as you are told. First there is the press conference. Then you go to the Great Britain house and sign the walls, you sign pictures and so on. There were a couple more interviews, and after that it was straight into the team car to go back to Foxhills to get ready for the time trial. It was overwhelming. I had joined Twitter a month earlier; I am a technophobe, so I had no idea what I was doing and I hadn't turned off my notifications or whatever they are. I had 20,000 messages – every man and his dog that I had ever been anywhere near in my life was contacting me – and I hadn't seen my family. My reaction was shock: 'I can't believe it's all over and I have an Olympic medal.'

We got back to the hotel. Chris was there and he pointed out, 'Obviously you have got the time trial coming up in a couple of days, so don't be too long.' My family had been put in a little room and they were all just waiting for me around the table; this would be my favourite memory from the Games. The kitchens had closed because it was so late by now, so there was no food, but my mum had had the foresight to save me a chocolate dessert because she knew I would want one. She made sure that I began eating, and then we had just the loveliest half hour together before I was told it was bedtime and they went and caught the last train home.

*   *   *

We had two clear days after the road race before the time trial, where I rode on my borrowed bike. Emma was super-focused and up for it, as she had taken silver in Beijing and won a world title two years earlier. My view was, 'Here we go, we'll see what happens.' All athletes deal with pressure in different ways and Emma and I are very different in our approach to everything.

When the pressure is on, I am a talker, Emma isn't. She radiates tension. If I get nervous, I talk more. That's how I always was as a team pursuiter. I would be lining up with Wendy and Jo; they would be silent for the day, and I would be jabbering away, finding anyone I could to talk to because

I don't like the pressure cooker. I don't believe in taking life too seriously, I like to act normal.

Physically I am best suited to making short, repeated efforts, recovering very quickly, rather than churning round a big gear at high speed, keeping going for a long time. That's probably why I don't find any enjoyment in time trials; because they are not my strong suit, I don't tend to bother much with them. To me, time trialling is a separate sport on its own compared to road racing. What I did like in London, however, was the day before the time trial, when we all rode round the circuit to get to know it, I was continually hearing people say, 'Well done.' I enjoyed that. I don't recall much about race day; I warmed up on my road bike as always, got on the time-trial bike on the rollers – I don't use a turbo as they give me a dead leg – I had Rod Ellingworth in the car behind me, and I came tenth.

The impact my medal made – the first home medal of the home games – had already began to trickle into me. Back in the hotel after the road race, we were in the bubble, so I didn't see any newspapers and I didn't watch the television. My sister sent me a picture of all the papers and then my mum and dad told me that they were going on TV with Rebecca Adlington's parents. That was hilarious. Rebecca's parents were almost media trained; mine were simply themselves.

The interviewer was asking Rebecca's parents about all the sacrifices they had made. They were saying, 'Yeah, we were up at six o'clock every morning to take her down to the pool.' Then they went to my mum and dad and asked the same question. They looked at each other and had a think and said, 'Wee-ell, er, we've worked on her confidence. We talk a lot about self-confidence and so on.' My dad sent me a text: 'Gary Lineker wears a lot of make-up.' I couldn't work out what he meant, but then I caught up and managed to watch it. It was surreal.

* * *

There were parts of the Games that I loved: watching sport and being with like-minded people. I wasn't keen on the London party scene, however. One night that August I was walking out of a nightclub and a cyclist I knew grabbed my hand. 'Oh, hiya,' I said, 'I haven't seen you for ages.' Then I realised she had latched on to me because there were photographers there, and holding my hand meant that we would be in the papers the next morning. I was aghast. Surely you are most proud of the medal you have just won, not who you got papped with when you were out partying?

After the time trial I was set free from the shackles of Foxhills. Escape wasn't straightforward; I had to wait in Hampton Court until the men's time trial was over before I could get a lift to the Olympic village. Meanwhile, getting over the road to where my parents were waiting without getting mobbed for autographs wasn't going to be easy. I put on my sunglasses and kept a low profile. I was doing fine until I saw Mum in a T-shirt saying, 'Go Lizzie.' There seemed to be hundreds of people, and I couldn't get away from them. It was a nightmare: I was trying to have a conversation with my mum and people kept jumping in with cameras as if they couldn't wait for ten seconds. They all wanted selfies: lots of them, selfie after selfie.

I spent two weeks in London on my own after the time trial, but the Olympic village experience that everyone talks about wasn't quite what I ended up with. That was a bit of a celebrity circuit, a weird place that wasn't my cup of tea. I was doing corporate work, staying in a hotel in Central London. It involved going to plenty of fun events but they were still corporate occasions – you turn up and put your best smile on – but it is not as if you are out with your best mates. You are rubbing shoulders with people who are acquaintances.

The most fun thing was watching the Andy Murray final at Wimbledon, even though I am a big fan of Federer. We got looked after, we did the whole high tea thing – it was lovely, a great day out, and then I got to go to Super Saturday at the Olympic Stadium and just be part of the crowd. The sporting element was what I liked, not the after-parties. By the end I was absolutely on my knees with exhaustion. I don't remember specifically why, but I do recall phoning my mum from a taxi as I travelled between events, and I cried down the phone at her. I was going from place to place for sponsors, journalists, VIPs, parties or what-ever, and I had had only half an hour after the race with my parents and the people who actually meant something to me.

It's hard to explain quite how knackered I was. By the end I just wanted to sleep for a single day, have no questions to answer, and not have to be excited. I just wanted to hide. I didn't really enjoy the experience because I would be sitting in a room full of athletes who hadn't achieved what they wanted to but who were delighted because they were at an after-party and someone from *The Only Way is Essex* was there was well. I kept thinking how odd it was, how great it would be if only my friends from home or my brother and sister were there. Then it would be a free party, free food, free booze and we could have a good time, but as it was I was stuck with people I didn't really know and probably wasn't going to have to see again.

My two weeks of 'living the life', as some people describe it, came to an end, and I was able to go where I most wanted to be: home. The homecoming in Otley was two days after the closing ceremony, the Tuesday; the Monday was a reception in Leeds with the Brownlees and the other Leeds medallists. The Yorkshire Helicopter Company offered to fly me and the Brownlees home from London, but because I am scared of helicopters I got a taxi home, which already felt like a luxury for me.

Back home in Otley the town council had asked my mum

and dad if they could put something on for me and I had said that it would be nice, so they had laid on an open-top bus. My mum had said, 'Oh, you can bring a couple of friends on the bus, and maybe Westy can come and make a speech, and then we'll have a party at home afterwards.' I distinctly remember being rather embarrassed because it started pouring with rain, so I told Mum to ring the town council and cancel the whole thing; it didn't make any difference. Because the whole idea was that local cyclists would ride behind the bus, the bus turned up and my street was choc-a-bloc with people on bikes getting soaked in the pouring rain. I was shocked. We set off down the hill from our house, did a lap of the town; it was packed. It was absolutely heaving with people standing in the pouring rain and there were signs up outside the pubs saying, 'Well done, Lizzie.'

The whole afternoon was incredible; a really, really lovely way to round off the Games. We had microphones and speakers set up on the top of the bus; Westy had a fairly long speech prepared but the town councillor spoke for what felt like an age, so it was a bit awkward. It was clear that any more speeches needed to be over quick because the crowd was getting restless, so he just said some nice things. I thanked all the local sports clubs, which had volunteers who had helped me get to this point. I signed a load of autographs and then we went home and had a party; we all had a great time. No selfies were taken.

CHAPTER 8

EQUALITY
AND POWER

During the run-up to the Olympic road race, I had been constantly reminded of the disparity between men and women in the British Cycling system. While staying in the Foxhills hotel I couldn't help thinking: 'Why am I paying, for my own electric gears? Why are there 20 staff for the male cyclists and only two for us?' On a more basic level, 'Why aren't we provided with the same bikes as the men?'

There were eight riders on the long-list for the men's road-race team: five to ride and three reserves. All eight were given new UKSI bikes, special aerodynamic carbon-fibre road machines based on the smoothed-out bikes that the track team had been using since before Beijing; they got the chance to test them beforehand. The men's road race was the day before our event, so we could have been offered the chance to use them as well – for example, I am the same size as Mark Cavendish.

We had the defending Olympic champion in Nicole Cooke and a silver medallist in Emma Pooley, but in terms of support we had nothing. If you compared our respective preparation for London – Cav's story and mine – it was like putting night next to day. We even had to ask to borrow aerodynamic helmets from Team Sky's helmet store; after the road race and time trial were over Lucy and I both received an email saying that if we didn't return the helmets we wouldn't be selected for the world championships. My view was, 'Oh yes, whatever, a helmet'; I wasn't intending to steal it. It felt bizarre.

It seemed that we were poor relations – the four of us sitting there, with everything going on around the men, Bradley and the Tour and the rest of it. We were using our own equipment, doing the best we could with what we had. The question that always crossed our minds concerned the funding from UK Sport. If the cash they put in was based on medals won, in what way did the money from the world championship medals won by Nicole and Emma during that Olympic cycle go towards furthering women's road racing? I don't know the answer. In terms of what was spent on me personally, I went on one training camp to Majorca and that was that for 2012.

This background might help to explain what I said at

the press conference immediately after the road race: 'It can get overwhelming and frustrating, the sexism I've experienced in my career. It's a big issue in women's sport. It's the obvious things: the salary, media coverage, the general things you have to cope with. If you focus on it too much, you get very disheartened.'

This was not premeditated. I didn't go in to the press conference, silver medal in hand thinking, 'Now, I'm going to say something', but I meant every word.

I remain proud of the fact that I came out and said what I did. I've always spoken up if I felt things needed changing. I've found myself in that position even though I'm not the campaigning type. I believe that what I had to say should have been only a small part of the press conference after the road race. I genuinely felt that the whole of London 2012 was so much bigger than any of the stuff I might have to say. I thought it would be a small corner of the papers the next day. I didn't expect any more than that. But it opened the floodgates. A lot more interviews were focused on equality after that, which was pretty overwhelming, and made the next few weeks quite hard-going.

The feeling went back further than the time I'd spent in Foxhills, obviously. I felt I had been fighting against sexism my entire career. I'd spent the previous year at Garmin trying to get myself on track and then suddenly their women's team had been disbanded at the end of the season, just like that. Meanwhile, it was business as usual for the men at Garmin.

I remember being really annoyed in 2007 in Sofia at the European road championships. I was racing everything that year; the women's team turned up at the race, the junior lads had just finished and were in the team tents cooling down. That meant the girls didn't have an area where we could warm up and just sit and get ready; it was a matter of, 'Get them boys out of here, our race is next.' We had to use sub-standard wheels while they were on good ones. It was little things like that, but it adds up over the years.

In London, I quickly got a sense that the agenda had run away from me, which made me more guarded when I was asked about equality issues in interviews, as I continually seemed to be after winning the silver medal. There were many journalists who didn't seem to understand why I shied away from discussing the issues in greater depth. The reason was that I had never experienced anything like this; it was strange to be reading things in the papers that put me in the limelight, and it felt very difficult to control the things that were being written about me.

My feeling towards campaigning is ambivalent to some extent. However much I may yearn for greater equality in women's racing, what I really want to do is ride my bike as fast as I can and let my results do the talking. Sometimes I simply don't have the extra energy available for campaigning, or the single-minded focus that you need for it, and I end up thinking, 'Why should it be me?' After my career is over I am more likely to have the time and the headspace to look into

– for example – the precise documentation of the women's World Tour. At the moment, I have to be selfish and think about myself. I don't believe people should expect me to turn up to every interview I do carrying a manifesto of how women's cycling should be improved.

I also wanted to remain myself and have no one else appropriate what I had said in order to further their own aims. Feminism can be controversial: my fear was that people who had more extreme beliefs than me, or had different views, would use what I had said to back up their personal agendas. And that in turn might mean that I would look as if I was a supporter of whatever they wanted to achieve. One journalist wrote that I was a reluctant campaigner, but that wasn't true. I had no issue with expressing my views, but I wanted to be the one who decided what I said and when. So to some extent, my reaction was to wind my neck in again.

*　*　*

Even while I was in the Olympic village in London I was trying to carry on training, because the silver medal had ignited my ambition to be world champion, and the course in Valkenburg, in the Netherlands, would suit me. It was just five weeks away. So I sat on the turbo trainer as often as I could, dead leg and all. However, I still had recurring stomach problems and couldn't find out what was the cause.

The symptoms pointed to something similar to IBS – it was incredibly painful – but we didn't begin to get the measure of it until I was actually at the world championships.

I was training with AA Drinks for the team time trial which opens the week's racing at the Worlds, staying in the same hotel as Team Sky. Richard Freeman, the GB team doctor, was there, so he assessed me and told me to go home and get it looked at in detail. The GB team booked the appointment and the guy who was running the logistics for GB came to my room to ask if I needed a room for later in the week, as we were in the same hotel in which GB would be staying for the road races. I said I needed a flight back to get to the doctor's for my stomach and his take was, 'Oh, AA Drinks will be covering that.' By this point, at the end of the women's season, AA were on a shoestring; the hotel was heaving with GB staff wearing Team Sky T-shirts, but GB couldn't afford to buy me a flight to Manchester.

When I did get to hospital, I was misdiagnosed with ulcerative colitis – it is a strain of a long-term immune disease, colitis, that leaves you with ulcers in the bowels. Steve Redgrave and Lewis Moody have both suffered from ulcerative colitis. I had various microscope tests to find out precisely what was going on and to try and determine whether I had Crohn's disease. I still felt under pressure to ride the Worlds, although I was so ill that I couldn't even have considered it. This is rarely overt; it's more people saying, 'You can ride, have some days off and then ride... People have done it in the past...' that sort of thing. But it took five weeks off the bike before I had recovered.

As had happened before, this took place against a background of uncertainty over team sponsorship. We had been told in August that AA Drinks would be pulling out, which at least gave us time to sort out some alternatives. Danny asked me what I wanted to do, whether I wanted to try and stick together with some of the other riders – several of the Dutch girls had gone straight to Rabobank, the biggest Dutch team – or if I had other options. There was a small group of us left, all out of contract, with nowhere to go. Eventually, Danny told us he had been in contact with a big cycling fan in Holland who was backing a club team and was looking to build it into something more substantial. It would be a bit of a gamble, but they wanted to offer me a good salary. He thought I should go for it; I thought, 'OK, trust a little bit here.'

The sponsor was Dolmans, a family-owned landscaping group. The owner is called Erwin Janssen, who is one of those well-got-up Dutch guys – they always look like James Bond, with lots of gel, matching scarf and handkerchief, and pointy shoes – but most importantly he's a massive fan of women's cycling. The team had been essentially Dutch club riders, with one Briton, Emma Trott; Lucy Martin and Jessie Daams came across with us. For 2013, the vehicle rental firm Boels came in, so this marked the start of the team that has developed with me over the past few years, giving me welcome stability.

* * *

That wasn't all that came out of 2012. That year, I was taught a valuable lesson about the pitfalls that lie out there when you are a female athlete. It was an episode that might also help to explain why I am reluctant to put my trust in people I don't really know well. We did a photoshoot for the *Evening Standard*, which was on a theme of Greek gods and goddesses, different Olympians in statuesque poses. They had a beautiful dress which I did some pictures in – really elegant, I loved it – but then they brought out a little pink leotard. I said, 'No, I don't want to be photographed in that.' They said, 'OK, fair enough, but just do it, we'll take one picture, see what you think. If you don't like it we won't use it.' I did that one picture, and that was the photo they used in the feature. It was a good lesson to learn: never, ever allow yourself to be photographed wearing something you are not comfortable with, or in a position you are not happy with, because you can't trust someone not to use that image.

I have always been utterly certain that I want to build my profile on my race results and performances rather than on the way I look. What I want is to be taken seriously – and I want women in sport to be taken seriously – because we are strong, rather than because of how we might look, or how we might be portrayed. I would read interviews or race reports that would say, 'Pretty Lizzie Armitstead wins this or that', or something of that kind, and I couldn't help thinking, 'Is that really necessary?' Of course it isn't.

There have been other instances where I have felt exploited. At one team photo shoot early in my career we had to do studio photographs, posing with various pieces of kit. The photographer had asked the girls to unzip their jerseys and so on, and I remember feeling very unhappy about it. My take on it was that we were a cycling team, I didn't understand why we were being asked to do this, and I didn't like it. There is a line that has to be drawn when it comes to your image, which is different for each athlete, and the point to draw it is when you start to feel uncomfortable.

It can be difficult to get these things right. Sometimes, being a woman as well as a cyclist, it would be nice to do a lifestyle shoot with a nice photograph in a dress. It is about showing enough femininity to make yourself happy with how the photo looks. Similarly, you have to look quite carefully at the kind of clothes you get asked to wear at awards ceremonies, where there will be various options. For example, Stella McCartney offered to dress me for the Sports Personality award; I had to think carefully about how I was going to dress and in the end I opted for something of hers that I liked. It's a question of what I feel comfortable in rather than what might increase my earning power. I wanted to look good and feel confident, but I didn't want to attract attention for the wrong reasons. For SPOTY if I had liked a short mini-dress I probably wouldn't have worn it, because I would have been likely to get headlines I didn't want.

There is pressure, and although it's not always overt, it is exerted directly through your earning power. In the age of social media, sponsors are attracted to athletes because of their profile. The question then is how you build that profile. I want it to happen through how I compete, rather than how I look or what photographs I chose to put on my social-media feeds. When I am deciding what pictures to upload to Twitter or Instagram I am consciously questioning, all the time, how much I should let people into my private life and how much of what happens around me I should put on display. I have always made the decision that the pictures have to be cycling-related in order for me to be authentic, and to be taken seriously.

The unfortunate truth is that if I uploaded an Instagram picture of me in a bikini, then it would end up making me money. Potential backers who are looking into whether they want to sponsor you will analyse your social-media following and say, for example, 'OK, if you have 300,000, then we will back you.' If you are going to do a photoshoot for *FHM* or *Nuts* in your underwear, then immediately you are going to get tagged and get a whole lot of new followers. That is how it works, but I am determined not to be a part of that.

There is another good example: *CyclePassion*. This is a

calendar where women cyclists from various nations are shot in provocative poses. There was one particular image that made my blood boil. It had two racing cyclists I knew in underwear and high heels, covered in oil, standing at the side of the road on an Alpine climb during the Tour de France while the men's professional peloton was racing past. My anger was centred on the fact that these women were not good cyclists but they were getting a high profile, and they just couldn't understand that they were being exploited. It infuriated me so much.

I get very annoyed when I see female athletes at the top of their sport taking their clothes off. They don't need to do it, and it undermines the rest of us. To me, being a woman in sport means not trading on your image, no matter how tempting or lucrative that could be. We need to stand together and refuse to do these things. They are simply not necessary.

There is another side to the body-image question, which is not specifically about cycling, but more generally about being a woman. Living in Monaco is difficult, because you are constantly surrounded by beautiful women whose whole life is centred around being attractive: they are very well manicured and there is a lot of plastic surgery in evidence. Growing up as a woman the images that are presented to you of the 'body beautiful' are not realistic or achievable.

That pressure is worse for an athlete because you are a public person and there are always photographs of you in circulation. I could think sometimes that I am too muscly, and therefore masculine, but that is just the sort of pressure that any normal woman has to live with; I am always determined not to fall into that trap.

At the moment, this pressure is also tied into social media. With Instagram and so on, people are becoming very self-obsessed and image-centred. Cycling is one of the most open sports there is in terms of access to the stars and the interaction between fans and athletes, but when you go to an event, people are less interested in asking me a question and finding out about what I do than they are in having a selfie taken with me so that they can put it online. They can talk to me, ask me something if they want, but the only contact they want is so that they can tell people they have had their photo taken.

It breaks my heart when I see young girls on the bus taking photographs of themselves. I think, You have got so much more to offer the world than a picture that you are filtering through social media. You can't filter your character. If people felt they were being judged on their personality rather than through what they can post on social media that would be far better. Let's hope it's only a phase and it passes.

Cycling has always been behind the curve in terms of gender equality. It took many years for women's events to be adopted at the Olympics – it didn't happen until 1984 – and even the road Worlds weren't open to women until 1958. Junior women didn't get a world championship until 1987 and there is still no under-23 world title in road or time trial for women. Gender parity on the track at the Olympics didn't happen until 2012; in 2017the men still had one more event at the track Worlds, the Madison, although women ride this discipline as well. There is a connection between the way women are depicted, and the history of the sport, which is institutionally sexist. The connection is simple: in both aspects, it is about taking women seriously, or not.

Another point that needs be made when we are looking at cycling and equality is that physically men and women are more equal than is usually accepted, although there is a big difference between the two sexes at elite level. A three-week Tour de France for women over the same distances as the men would be perfectly feasible if there were a good number of nine-women teams competing, all of whom had athletes on a minimum wage and who had the same opportunity to train as the men. As it is, there is still too much of a disparity within the women's peloton in earning power and fitness for that to work.

You only have to look back to the second half of the 2oth century to my fellow Yorkshirewoman Beryl Burton, who took the 12-hour record for men and women, to realise that on two wheels women are not inherently physically weaker than men. Having said that, a 12-hour time trial is totally different to a road race over, say, 140km. I could perhaps survive in a men's road race, but I wouldn't come close to the best.

What I do know from training with male professional

cyclists is that we are not so very different. My husband Philip Deignan, is training to race as a domestique with Team Sky for three-week Tours; he is doing 25-hour weeks on his bike. I am doing 18–20 hours. I am a different kind of rider – a Classics rider rather than a climber – so it is difficult to compare us directly, but in terms of my peak power output, it is higher than Phil's, although he would beat me on a climb: I am faster than him, because I am lighter as well. I know I am not far off the threshold power of some of the male sprinters.

That said, women cyclists don't need to make comparisons with the men in order to be taken seriously. To me, one of the problems facing our sport is that we constantly have to justify ourselves compared to how the men perform, but that is always going to be a losing argument. There will be aspects of performance where there is a closer crossover than people might think – for example my peak power being higher than Phil's – but overall, women cannot compete with men. My colleague Elisa Longo Borghini summed up how I feel in an interview, which I want to quote:

We women are athletes. We train and we race and we eat and we sleep and we live as professional athletes. We do nothing less than the men. I don't know why people can't understand that because women can't achieve the exact same thing as men or against men that we are still achieving something very hard and very great...

This might come as a surprise to some, but we don't want to be men. We are happy to be women. It doesn't matter to us that we might be less fast or less strong, because our bodies are built differently. I want to have children one day. I don't want to ride 250 kilometres every weekend. My body is built differently to a man's, but why is it that I can't have the same reward, the same pride, the same respect?

The Tour of Flanders is such an important race for the whole peloton – for men, and for women. The same skills the men show going over the Koppenberg, the women need to get up the Kwaremont. Why does it matter that we might be a bit slower? What is the problem with this? Why can't we compete only with our own sex? If we can't compete with men, does that mean we can't compete at all?

On the bike, it is always satisfying to prove men wrong, particularly male professionals. If I go out training with men – as I sometimes do from Monaco and Nice, where many male pros are based – there are rides when they keep looking round to check whether I am still there. They always looked shocked whereas I just smile. When I first got together with Phil he said something to me along the lines of, 'What, you go out on your bike for four hours?' I rolled my eyes in frustration. Of course I do.

CHAPTER 9

YEAR
OF DOOM

It took more than a year for the Olympic hangover to settle, which is why I think of 2013 as the year of doom. My form was terrible, I struggled to find a bike from my new sponsor that fitted me properly, the team didn't gel together well and I never truly got going. Looking back, I had probably been to too many dinners and parties over the winter, but that didn't mean I had been lazy. I had continued to train hard; the issue was that I had been doing too much and not resting up enough. What really slowed me down, however, was that I spent most of 2013 fighting through feelings of cramp and pain high up in my stomach.

Everyone gets cramp, most often in their calves; I would experience intense pain exactly as if I was cramping up, but in my stomach, and it would remain painful in that area for another couple of days or more after each attack. I felt as if I was chasing form for the entire season. When that happens, you never have the confidence to take the rest that you need to recover; you end up over-training and enter a negative spiral. The upshot was that I had one satisfying result in the entire year: gold in the national championship road race, held on the course in Glasgow that was to be used for the Commonwealth Games. The race was a wearing-down process, with the field reduced each time on the main hill until I finally had just two riders to worry about: Dani King and Laura Trott, both from the Wiggle-Honda team. The only solution was to attack last time up the climb; fortunately it worked.

The world championships in Florence went terribly, an occasion more marked due to the high expectations following the silver medal in London. I would love to race on that course now because it's demanding and tactically interesting, but on the day I was in a lot of pain from my stomach. During the race I was sick about ten times; at one point a Polish girl came and asked if I was all right. I thought, 'It's the world championships. It's very nice of you to ask, but I wouldn't be asking you that.' It was a bit frustrating being constantly asked how I was getting on. I just wanted people to leave me to get on with it. I went on a gluten-free diet for most of the year to try and figure out if being coeliac was what lay behind my troubles. That runs in the family – my mum, my granddad and my uncle are all coeliac – so there was a fair chance that it was either that or some kind of intolerance that the doctors weren't picking up. So I gave it a go, but eventually I cracked and had a big pizza after the world championship. It tasted like heaven as I'd not eaten gluten all year. I had no reaction to the pizza, so I figured I wasn't intolerant after all.

We finally got on top of the stomach problems during the early autumn when I went to see a doctor at Blackburn hospital. He did a test on me where you drink something and then they rotate you upside down on a machine to see how your oesophagus functions. What they worked out from this was that the lower part of my oesophagus doesn't work correctly because my stomach sits up three centimetres into the oesophagus. There's a sphincter muscle at the top which means things should go in rather than out, but mine doesn't function, hence the vomiting: obviously when you are riding the bike you spend a lot of time bent over, so I would be sick quite frequently. There was also the fact that my stomach doesn't empty properly, because the tube that empties out of it is situated in the middle of the stomach. That causes inflammation and acid reflux, which is like having heartburn all the time. Plus, the stress related to all of that caused irritable bowel syndrome.

I was prescribed Lansaprazole, which is a basic anti-acid, and a sort of laxative – metoclopramide – which relaxes the stomach, but crucially I have learnt to be very cautious with my stomach. If I have spells when it is flaring up, which it unfortunately does when I am stressed out, then I have to back off. But simply knowing what was up with me helped a huge amount.

* * *

With equality high up the agenda after the London Games, Florence saw a change at the top of the Union Cycliste Internationale (UCI), the body that runs the sport worldwide, with the British nominee Brian Cookson taking over from the Irishman Pat McQuaid. Working to develop women's cycling was on Brian's agenda, which was a step forward from what had gone before. There have been some improvements in the support we receive from the UCI since Brian's election – equal prize money at the world championships, the new women's World Tour – but I have yet to see any game-changing innovations.

Another way in which equality began to filter through was in the campaign for the relaunch of a women's Tour de France alongside the men's event, which drew nearly 100,000 signatures to an online petition, and eventually prompted the Tour de France organisers to run La Course – a women's criterium on the Champs-Elysées as a prelude to the finish of the men's race on the final Sunday. The Tour of Spain – which is run by a Spanish offshoot of the same company – followed suit by doing a similar event on the closing day of the Vuelta.

Although they are prestigious events, there is a frustrating side to races like La Course and the equivalent held after the Vuelta, the Madrid Challenge. I find speaking to the media about these events one of the hardest things to get right because they feel like a token gesture to me, but I receive a lot of media attention based around them. These events have iconic backdrops, they are a massive stage for us, and unlike some circuit races I am asked to ride, they do have corners. But I wouldn't dream of resting up midweek to ride them fresh. In racing terms, they are a bit difficult because I have to turn into a bunch sprinter at these events, and that is no longer my strongest suit. So when I don't win, the headlines are 'Armitstead only fourth: is she losing form?'

To date, La Course has not felt like a game-changer, even though for 2017 it was changed to a brief version of one of the Tour's Alpine stages. I didn't feel I could make the early editions a major target because it was essentially a criterium, albeit one in a spectacular setting with a huge crowd and it wasn't a great preparation race for anything more major. It felt like an event we had to go to Paris for, and I struggled with that. I don't know how much impact it has had on the bigger picture of women's racing.

When it comes to running a women's Tour alongside the men's event, as they did in the 1980s, I can totally understand the logistical issues that worry the organisers; it wouldn't be easy to put on two three-week Tours at the same time on the same roads. However, I do think it would be possible to organise at least one decent race for women alongside these events. If you look at the way the women's Tour de Yorkshire has developed, they started off with an event on an easy circuit, which I didn't want to ride because there was nothing appealing about it, but 12 months later they moved to a full road race held on the same course as one of the stages in their men's three-day. Let's face it: starting in Otley they might have had a backlash from the locals if they hadn't had a women's race. And they put up an immense prize list, more than equal with the men, but what made me more pleased was that they provided a proper length race over a real road course – as a rider, you want to know that you have actually earned that equal prize money.

Another question that began to come up more frequently was whether Team Sky should have set up a women's team alongside their men's squad when that was started in 2010. The cost would have been relatively minimal – perhaps half a million pounds compared to their budget of over £30 million – and it would have set an example to others, as well as providing a focus for the British women, and sitting well alongside other activities they sponsored such as the women-only Breeze rides. Part of me says that they should have done it, although personally I'm not sure I would have ridden for them in any case given how well things have worked out with Boels-Dolmans. Boels-Dolmans have given me valuable stability during the full Olympic cycle between

London and Rio, plus the opportunity to work with Danny, who has been key to my success.

It wouldn't have been that straightforward for British Cycling to set up a women's squad alongside Sky from nothing. They would have needed an infusion of new staff to run it, and they probably would have been doing it largely because of media and political pressure, the need to be seen to be forward-thinking and not to be sexist. I'm happy where I am, in a squad where the sponsor and staff have been behind us from the beginning, rather than riding for someone who has felt coerced into setting up a team for me.

Another question is whether to oblige men's World Tour teams to run a women's squad alongside their men's set-up as a condition of having World Tour status. I don't know the answer to this because I have seen two sides to it. On the face of it, this is the simplest and best solution. The good experience I had at Cervélo is an obvious argument for doing it; I've also been told that for some WorldTour teams finding the half a million pounds it would take could be achieved simply by tightening up on logistics. On the other side of the coin, Garmin in 2011 was a bad experience, showing what happens when a men's team has no option but to run a women's squad. However, the bottom line is that no matter how much Garmin may have been paying lip service to the idea of supporting women, the women riding for them had better provision than in many other women's teams.

The only straightforward way in which women's cycling can move ahead across the board is through the introduction of a minimum wage. The depth of talent in the peloton is increasing year on year. Every year it gets harder to win races – Marianne Vos found that in 2013 – and every year there are more riders in the peloton who are capable of winning the best events, but behind that top tier the level drops off quickly. So in order for the second-tier riders to improve, they need to be paid a wage that provides enough for them to focus solely on cycling rather than having to work alongside their training and racing or rely on their families for support.

My off-the-cuff guess would be that about half the riders in the women's peloton riding UCI events are unpaid. A minimum wage of 20,000 euros per year would make all the difference, not because the riders receiving it would get rich, but because they would have enough to live off, with expenses from their teams. That disparity in ability means that organisers are inclined to protect the back of the peloton rather than giving the riders at the front the chance to show what we can do. If you ran a stage of the women's Giro d'Italia over a massive, iconic climb such as the Gavia, there would be only ten riders in the front group, which isn't what people want to see. I can understand that you have to protect the grass roots and give the teams that are down the pecking order a chance, but it is holding the sport back. The lack of depth gives race organisers a dilemma: they are afraid of running events over the hardest courses because they may end up with races that aren't dramatic, but if they send their fields over easy courses the races won't be dramatic either.

That's not the biggest issue we as women face, however, in terms of races. In 2013 there were major concerns about the standard of the races we were being asked to ride. That year, my team pulled out of two events, the Tour of Tuscany and the Tour of Languedoc, due to concerns over safety. Tuscany was scary: we were going between two lines of open traffic as if we were commuting to work but with numbers on our backs. There was a protected 'window' for the break of six, but everyone else had to fend for themselves. This was a race that carried *hors categorie* status, the highest awarded by the UCI, but it was worse than riding a third-category race in England, because the cars were in front of us, in the lane of the road that we were using. We were not that far behind the front group, but we were completely left to our own devices.

In Languedoc the problem was subtly different: the organisers couldn't guarantee that they had enough police on hand to make for a safe race, so our team and Rabobank – Marianne Vos's squad – didn't start. It actually ended up being a nice week, curiously enough; we went and stayed in a random house in the middle of rural France and rode up Mont Ventoux. Other teams did keep racing, however, which I can empathise with to some degree: they had people there who had taken a week off work to help out at a bike race. I can understand the organisers' position as well, because they are dedicated people – the ones who run the Tour of Tuscany had been doing it for 15 years – but I don't understand what goes on in their minds, because Tuscany is actually a memorial race for a rider, Michela Fanini, who was killed by a car. We are professionals and we have to have minimum standards.

The problem is that you have riders who will be willing to race no matter what the conditions, as was the case in Tuscany. I am always among the first to visualise what can happen, and say no, because I have first-hand experience of what the worst-case scenario might be. The year I won the best young rider's jersey at the Giro – 2009 – the organisers cancelled the final stage, which was on a circuit where the roads weren't closed properly. I remember a girl crashing due to a pothole, going into the side of a wall, and her body just going limp. Every time we passed that spot the ambulance was still there with her. The Russians still wanted to race, though; they were attacking even as we abandoned. That has stuck with me.

As professionals we face a wider spectrum of conditions within races than our male counterparts. Generally, for World Cup races the standard is high: a team presentation the day before in whatever town we are based, a proper podium ceremony at the start, and all the paraphernalia you would expect: motorbikes, radios, a proper podium at the finish and photographers on the line. There are also really good events, like the Thüringen Rundfahrt in Germany where you stay in the same hotel and travel to the stages. You know that the hotel will be good, the food will be fine, and that makes up for the fact that the transfers may be a bit long. On the other hand, there are still times when I go to a UCI-ranked race and the start is in a car park without showers or toilets or any facilities. There are still races – particularly in France – where you sleep in school dormitories. It sounds obvious, but we need minimum standards across UCI-ranked races.

*   *   *

At the start of 2014 my relationship with Adam finally came to an end. It had been turbulent – we had split up and got back together time after time over our eight years together – and eventually the final straw came while he was in Australia early in the season. I decided enough was enough, packed up all my stuff in the apartment in Monaco, wrote him an email to tell him I was leaving. When we had parted previously it had always been in the back of my mind that it wasn't going to be for ever, but this time I knew it was final.

It felt similar to when I had walked out of the velodrome after giving up track racing: I was petrified, but I was sure it was the right decision. It ended up being a defining moment in my career and my life. I felt incredibly hurt. I had invested so much in this relationship. I am a very loyal person and the hurt came from the fact that someone in whom I had invested so much and to whom I had showed loyalty had

171

repaid that by causing me pain. I wanted to be at home with my family.

Although my parents didn't run around after me early on in my cycling career, they are only a phone call away if I really need them. So I did what I always do in a crisis and called my father: 'Dad, I need to leave.' He organised a rental car for me, a Renault Espace, and I fitted my entire life into it in secret, because I knew if I told any of my friends in Monaco they would try to persuade me to stay. The only friend who knew was Tiffany Cromwell, a fellow cyclist, who helped me put everything together, helped me back up the car, and gave me supplies of chocolate for the drive. I absolutely needed to leave.

It was a massively intense time, but the real hurt only lasted about three weeks. Adam and I had started going out when we were both just 16 and had grown into different people by the time we reached our early 20s. Our lives were intertwined, which made it like a divorce; I was no longer part of that two-person team we had been. Over the years, I had turned into someone else, but I was trying not to be that person, because it didn't fit with the direction in which Adam had gone.

There had been huge changes for both of us, and moving to Monaco had highlighted that. Adam loved Monaco for the reasons that I struggle with it sometimes: the glamour, the glitz and the famous people you rub shoulders with. What I like about it is the sunshine, the nice food, having mountains to train in – although not to race in – and the 'bubble' side of it, which means that you can come here and be totally focused on cycling, with no distractions. Although I am very boring in the way I live when I'm not on my bike, in Monaco I have the chance to look out of the window and see plenty going on, and there is always people-watching to do. Compared to Belgium, where we lived in a very sleepy village, there is a lot happening right on your doorstep.

I picked up 700 euros worth of speeding tickets on the way to Paris, where I had a rendezvous with my dad at a hotel in Disneyland Paris, which was so awful it was hilarious. I swear someone had put sugar in the air-conditioning: the air in the room smelt so sweet, sticky and cheap. I had three chocolate Magnums for dinner, we switched all my bits and pieces from the rental car to Dad's car, and then got stuck for a good two hours trying to return the hire car in Disneyland.

In the long term, the break-up was liberating; I would be able to be confident in the things I believed in, and in the person that I am. In the short term, I grew up a lot in a very brief space of time. Dad and I made it back to Yorkshire on the Tuesday before Het Nieuwsblad, which marks the beginning of the European racing season. I moved back into my parents' house, put all my stuff in the spare bedroom and then set off for Nieuwsblad, completely shattered but totally on a mission. There, I made probably the longest break the race has ever seen and finished third behind Amy Pieters and Emma Johansson, with the bunch right on our heels.

Racing without Adam was important and probably helped to speed up the healing process. As I often find at difficult times, it helped to ride my bike for escape and distraction, but there was something else: Adam and my racing were so bound together that I had rarely competed completely on my own account. When I had started racing, I wanted to do better because I fancied him and he was on the Talent Team as well; later, his family were always the ones with the kit who knew more about cycling than I did and I wanted to live up to that. Racing had been part of the identity of our relationship, so competing as a single woman was a significant statement. Later, I also realised that you see a lot of people within relationships who don't let their talent shine, and hold their personality back to placate their partner's ego; I had rarely allowed myself to celebrate my victories because Adam had needed results more than I did, and his racing had been more of a priority than mine.

After Nieuwsblad, I went back to Otley for about a week before I came to the conclusion that there was no way I would be able to live in the UK if I wanted to take my cycling seriously. It dawned on me that there was no reason why I should give up the life that I had made in Monaco and which I liked. I had friends there, and everything I needed. So I began coming back to stay in people's apartments here and there while I started to look for somewhere of my own to live. To begin with I hadn't imagined that I would be able to afford it, but I soon realised how much less money I was going to spend being single. I had actually been in a position where I didn't really understand my own finances.

It wasn't easy finding an apartment, doing all the work in a foreign language and looking at places on the Internet when I was away at races. Eventually, you have just got to get lucky. My estate agent showed me the apartment I ended up choosing by email before it actually went on the market, so I rented it unseen. Finding somewhere to live in Monaco is peculiar, because a lot of people have places there purely to claim residency for tax purposes, rather than in order to live there. As a result, you can be offered somewhere that costs three and a half thousand euros a month to rent but where the toilets are held together by masking tape. Or you can find an apartment you can live in, with a bit of a view, which is what I ended up with.

I had to figure all this out pretty rapidly, while dealing with French contracts, transferring money, putting down deposits and buying furniture. I hired another van and drove to Ikea in Toulon and bought everything I needed. Paul and Laura di Resta were fantastic friends throughout this period; they came to Ikea on the pretence that they needed things as well, but I suspect that what they bought fitted in the footwell between me and Laura. I then stayed up two nights in a row putting everything together before someone lent me an electric drill, after which it all went along much faster. I needed to turn things around quickly, because all the upheaval in my private life was starting to tire me out.

I enjoyed decorating the apartment exactly how I wanted it, without compromising to account for another person's taste. I set everything up, moved into my new place, and then looked after myself for the next few months. I felt like an adult for the first time.

CHAPTER 10

ALL CHANGE

On the climb of Great George Street in Glasgow on 3 August 2014 I had a decision to make, and I had to make it fast. Emma Pooley had attacked in the Commonwealth Games road race and had a gap as we hit the one-in-seven slope. Ten kilometres to go: my legs felt good and I had never felt under any pressure during the last two hours. It felt easier in the race than it had in training. What to do? Emma was my teammate with the England squad, wearing the cross of Saint George like me. She was clearly in sight, 50 metres up ahead on the one-in-seven climb, and well within catching distance if I went for it. Now. As professional athletes we are not paid to chase down our teammates. That is not how it works.

While Emma and I were preparing for the road race, we

were sharing a house in the athletes' village, and talking about our futures. Emma had told me about her impending retirement from international cycling, her aims after that, her move into triathlon and duathlon. She had even been running that week. But I was taking no prisoners, not even if they were teammates. At that precise moment, I thought, 'I wouldn't have dreamt of going running before this race. For the last two weeks I have not even allowed myself to walk around the supermarket. I have put everything into this race. I want this more than you.'

I flew past Emma 100 metres before the top of the climb, and rode the final eight kilometres to the finish alone. Afterwards, with the gold medal around my neck, it felt good. I had no second thoughts, however much and in whatever terms Emma's fans might express their disapproval on Twitter. Emma seemed happy with the silver medal, delighted even, although she didn't say anything. I had been the best on the day. Had we been on opposing teams, with Emma racing against me, there is no way she would have got away from me on that course, or outsprinted me. It was the first time in my career that I had been ruthless. And I was comfortable with it.

* * *

Much of the time, the secret ingredient in success is self-belief. Through 2014, after my relationship with Adam had finally come to an end, I became a much more confident person. As a single woman that year I learnt a lot about myself. I finally understood that I did like my job and I wasn't only racing a bike because I was part of a package where Adam cycled and I cycled and that was how it had always been. The person I had been in my relationship with Adam didn't match the person I am. I am not someone who compromises easily, but for a long time I had been willing to accept certain things that I wouldn't stand for now. I had felt that I was carrying us both, rather than it being mutually supportive.

Now, I was independent and for the first time ever I was concentrating solely on myself as a cyclist. Due to the nature of our relationship I had been looking after Adam and motivating him, never completely realising that it is very tiring to take care of two people's motivation and two people's nutrition and two people's finances and so on. Now in terms of cycling it was only about me, and my thought process followed this sequence: if I am going to do this, I am going to do it properly. I am not going to compromise anything for anyone else any more. It was a complete turn-around. In the period I was single I think I flourished because I was finally able to be selfish and just take care of myself.

At the start of the season I flew because I was angry, I was going well, and I was probably skinnier than usual because I hadn't eaten much for six weeks. It was a lethally good combination if you wanted to compete at the highest level.

The Ronde van het Hageland at Tielt-Winge will always be a race with massive significance for me because it falls on the anniversary of my uncle's death, and he died in 2012, the year I first won it. No matter what kind of mood I am in, I always race well there, and in 2014 I won it again. Then it was on to the Ronde van Drenthe, the first round of the World Cup, where the main obstacle is a man-made climb tracking over what used to be a rubbish dump. It's a key event for us every year, as our backers Boels sponsor it as well, so we have to perform.

The team had moved on again over the winter, completing the transition from club team to senior player in the peloton. Boels had already joined Dolmans for 2013, but over the winter we had got Specialized on board and we had signed Ellen van Dijk – a really strong Dutchwoman – and the American Megan Guarnier, who was to ride really well in 2015 and 2016. Ellen played a key role in my win in Drenthe: the break, Iris Slappendel and Anna van der Breggen, was a minute ahead after the peloton had gone off course, and at the key moment before the main climb, Danny came to me on the radio and said, 'Lizzie, how do you feel?'

'I feel really, really good.'

Then he gave Ellen her instructions: 'Ellen, you have to ride to the climb, or you will lose the break.'

Ellen brought Iris and Anna back to 20 seconds at the foot of the climb, she dropped me off there, I attacked, caught Anna and then outsprinted her – wow! Two wins in two weeks. The team was delighted: we all shared champagne with the sponsors afterwards. That was lovely, but it wouldn't happen now; they are more used to big wins. The grandfather of the company, the guy who had owned Dolmans from day one, was talking away to me in Dutch and giving me far too many kisses. He was so delighted. I'd been moving house as well, so it was a busy time all round.

What had changed in 2014 was that for the first time, I went to the biggest races and tried to win them. I ended up in first place overall in the World Cup, which was good, but I didn't win another round after Drenthe, which was frustrating. I wanted to win more. People tend to put goals in your mouth; I never dreamt of winning the World Cup, of being dominant or consistent enough over an entire season to do that. What appealed to me was winning the biggest races: the one-day events on the women's calendar that have a bit of history about them. That led to a bit of a disconnect. At every World Cup round I went to, the same question was asked: Will Lizzie keep the leader's jersey or not? I wasn't really interested. I genuinely wanted to win the individual races. The leader's jersey was the by-product of almost winning, and doing so several times over.

The margin between winning and coming second can be very narrow, and often it's as much mental as physical. The Binda Trophy at Cittiglio on Lago Maggiore is a beautiful event, run by a small organisation of passionate Italian cyclists who put their heart and soul into it. It is slightly different to most of the early-season races; they tend to be suited to Classics-type riders, all-rounders like me, whereas Binda is one for the lightweights, with a long climb on the initial loop, followed by a couple of ascents on the finish circuit – a short steep one then a two-kilometre drag – and not much recovery between them. That profile means that riders often skip it between the Belgian races, and for the climbers, it's used as a bit of an early-season test: Emma Pooley is a past winner, for example.

That March, I came second to Emma Johansson, thanks to a single error: I started my sprint too late even though I was the fastest of the eight-rider lead group. It came down to confidence: even though I had won the Ronde van Drenthe convincingly I still didn't believe in myself when it came to winning World Cups. I still thought I was aiming for the first three. You have to trust your instinct when it comes to sprinting, or rather when it comes to sensing the right moment to start your sprint. I didn't have that yet.

I finished second, again, at the Tour of Flanders, but this was different. It was a solo victory for Ellen, where I marked the chase group behind her before outsprinting them to give us a 1–2, which rewarded her for the work she had done in Drenthe. As far as I was concerned, I had moved on massively: I was able to ride the most prestigious spring Classic in complete control, never feeling like I was under pressure or might be dropped.

I miscalculated my sprint again at Flèche Wallonne, which comes later in April, a couple of weeks after Flanders. Flèche has a tough, hilly course, with the same super-steep finish up the Mur de Huy that is used by the men's race later in the day. It doesn't pan out like the men's race, which is a single rush to the foot of the climb for the last time; at the women's Flèche the peloton tends to be in pieces before the final climb because there are so many hills beforehand. It's another climber's race, but the main reason I struggle with it is that it comes so soon after Flanders, which is usually my biggest objective for the spring. Two weeks doesn't sound long to maintain your focus, but when you have been training all winter for one goal, it can seem that way.

To win Flèche, I need to keep training hard after Flanders, and to do that I have to be both physically and mentally strong beforehand and then I have to be in top mental shape on the day, because physically it's not suited to me. I have the power to get over the climbs, but I need to fight all the way, to really want it. I am capable of winning it, but the pressure I am under beforehand makes it tough, so it's a love–hate relationship. I led the whole way up the Mur, going at the speed that suited me and avoiding the rush of riders from behind. I hung on for as long as I could, but without ever thinking that I could win it. Afterwards, having finished second, I realised that I had been stronger than I had thought and I had actually provided Pauline Ferrand-Prévot of France with the perfect lead-out. At the bottom of the hill I was aiming for the top ten; ten metres after the line I was already thinking I could have won.

On the bike, throughout the year there was another significant change. When I had been with Adam we used to go out on our bikes together all the time. We would ride with his teammates who lived in Monaco – mainly the Belgian pro Philippe Gilbert and the Norwegian sprinter Thor Hushovd – and sometimes the drivers from Formula One and motorbike racing who are based there. Going out on my own, I realised that that hadn't been great for me, because I would rarely be 'in the wind' – riding in the shelter provided by the men I might go quicker, but I would work less. Also, I would tend to follow their programme, which was dictated by what races they were riding: I never actually planned properly what I needed to do. As a single person I ended up going on fewer coffee rides with the drivers, and consequently planned my training properly. Another spin-off was that my diet improved because I ate out a lot less often. I went from going to a restaurant two or three times a week to perhaps once a fortnight, which helped when it came to paying off the mortgage and as an athlete it gave me more control over what I was eating.

It took a while for me to concentrate on winning rather than finishing on the podium. That step-change comes down partly to physiological maturity but is mainly a question of confidence, of believing in your ability to do different things. I had come from track racing and had always been labelled a sprinter. As it actually happened, I didn't like bunch sprints, but even so I was recognised as a fast finisher. However, when I had won points races on the track, that hadn't happened so much because I was a sprinter as because I had a bigger engine than the other riders: that meant I was capable of taking points towards the end of the race when everyone else was getting tired. Going into Flèche Wallonne in 2014 I had thought, 'This is ridiculous, I can't win this, I am a sprinter', and that was what happened. The critical thing was to learn that I was not still in the pigeonhole I had been given when I was 16 years old.

There were frustrations in the first part of that year. The women's Tour of Britain was run that spring for the first time. Radically, for a women's race, the organisers wanted to start from the idea that women would race under precisely the same conditions as in their men's race: identical prize money, the same standard of road closure and the same accommodation. It didn't work out in one way; the stages were mainly flat, and they weren't particularly long, given that we are capable of racing over 130 kilometres. It didn't make for a great spectacle, and it didn't showcase what women are capable of. Initially, I couldn't work out why the course was so undemanding until it became obvious that they had club teams in the race who wouldn't be capable of hanging on to the elite group at the front, but this is something underlines what I said in the previous chapter about the need for higher standards.

As an event, the women's Tour was great to be a part of. I felt very proud seeing the massive crowds who turned out for us; people simply couldn't believe how many there were. It had an Olympic feeling about it, fans by the roadsides waving their Great Britain flags. Riders from other nations, people from other teams, kept coming up to me and saying how impressed they were. And from a team perspective it was the first time we had had proper video footage of the finishes so that we could analyse our sprint lead-outs; we would watch the television highlights in the evening and work out where we went wrong. In most events it's impossible to learn because you don't have the overhead images from a helicopter to look at, so it's clear where everyone is; at best you have footage from a motorbike sitting just ahead of the peloton. You can't learn from that.

Britain stands out as the best race I have ever ridden, in terms of organisation: the nicest hotels, the most media coverage, even press conferences, which we don't normally have at most races. Personally, however, it was a frustrating week in terms of results. I was going pretty well, picking up time bonus seconds in the intermediate sprints ahead of Marianne Vos, so my speed was there, but as a team we never quite got it together in the finish sprints. There was one particularly rainy day and after that I came down with stomach issues again, and I had no option but to abandon.

Going into the Commonwealth Games in Glasgow, there was a thought at the back of my mind. I had always had this particular idea, and it was a deep-rooted one: I am going to be one of those people who is unlucky. I am going to be one of those people who never win on the big days. I had had so many silver medals throughout my career in all sorts of disciplines and all sorts of events. However, that is a self-fulfilling prophecy: if you think you are unlucky and won't win gold, that is what will happen. I now believe that I had to endure the frustration of all those second places to make myself change mentally. You need to change the way you think, and say to yourself: 'Hang on, I'm sacrificing just as much as the others. If I can make that mental switch, the silver medals can become gold medals without that much more effort.'

Before Glasgow I had to ride La Course in Paris, and I crashed, a really hard one, right into the barriers at full pelt. That left me with a big gash in my elbow, one that needed stitches, but luckily nothing was broken – I'm told I have good bone density, touch wood. That crash happened two weeks out from the Commonwealth Games; I was down to ride the time trial, which was another selection that I wasn't bothered about, so I pulled myself out and thought, 'Right, I'll concentrate only on the road race.'

I knew the course, obviously, from winning the national championship there the year before, and in Glasgow, on the day, everything fell into place. It was raining, the only day's rain during the whole of the Games, which as in London was perfect for me. It was an early start, 8:30 in the morning, so everyone was getting up to have breakfast the regulation three hours before, at 5:30am. I got up at 6:30am and had breakfast on my own, applying a little bit of common sense and experience in my approach. The race felt small, almost amateur, because the pool of riders in the Commonwealth is relatively small; there was a clear moment in the 99 kilometres when I had to make a decision, and I made the right call at the right time. On the day, I made that winning attack in precisely the same spot where I had left Laura and Dani 13 months earlier.

*   *   *

The racing wasn't the only part of my life that seemed to be falling into place as the year progressed. Splitting up with Adam had changed the dynamics of some of my most significant relationships. It had strengthened my bond with my sister, because she hadn't trusted Adam; the two of us are very close, so when Adam and I parted, that relationship improved again. My friendship with Tiffany Cromwell also blossomed; Tiffany had moved to Cap d'Ail, a few hundred metres over the border into France, to be with her then boyfriend Richie Porte, like Adam a professional on the road. When she split up with Richie, and I parted company with Adam, we became closer; when I moved out, she was the only person in Monaco that I told.

I wouldn't say I don't want friendships within cycling; it's

ELIZABETH
THE
SECOND

FREE INSIDE
GIANT POSTER
ZARA'S OLYMPIC
DEBUT

The day after winning Great Britain's first Olympic medal I was front page of the Times,
the start of many surreal moments of the 2012 Games.

© News Syndicate

Above: Posing with my medal outside St Paul's. This was the start of a busy but exciting two weeks in London, carrying my medal with me everywhere.

Below: Joanna Rowsell (now Rowsell-Shand) and I feeling incredibly proud and happy after winning Olympic medals and enjoying the closing ceremony in London. Competing in different disciplines but understanding each other's journey to get there makes my friendship with Joanna special.

Left: Winning a title solo is not a tactic I can normally execute: the Commonwealth Games was a masterpiece.

© Getty Images

Right: Fraternising with the enemy, always in competition with each other but more firmly friends. Australian Tiffany Cromwell and I on a 'food hall date' at the Commonwealth Games.

Top left: The moment I became World Champion was the only thing I hadn't planned to perfection; if I had, this wouldn't have been my winning salute.

© *Rex Featur*

Top right and bottom: Giving all I have got to make sure I cross that finish line first.

© *Cor*

Left: Listening to the
National Anthem
holding my medal,
trying to take
everything in so that
I didn't forget any
of it.

Right: My brother
in law always used
to laugh at my
feeble champagne
celebration, but
after some practise I
seem to have learned
how to milk the
celebrations.

Below: Giving Danny a big hug. It was around an hour after finishing the World
Championship race that I finally got to see him and thank him.

Above: After years of trying and an epic effort I finally crossed the finish line first in the Tour of Flanders in 2016.

© Getty Image

Below: Here I am during a recon of the Olympic Road Race course in August 2015. I was daunted by the prospect of racing up to this vista.

bove: All smiles alongside Evelyn Stevens, Megan Guarnier and Christine Majerus. I
ad just won the Philadelphia World Cup despite feeling incredibly jet lagged, I really
njoyed my first experience of racing in America. *(© Corvus)*

elow: An impromptu dedication to Evelyn at the finish line of her last professional race.
vie' was a great friend and teammate, an inspirational woman in many ways. *(© Corvus)*

Left: Philip proposed on his birthday during a picnic on top of a local mountain. Pure happiness!

Right: Mr and Mrs Deignan.

more that I haven't tended to pursue them. I started cycling later than most, so my friendships in cycling would have developed later; I already had a circle of friends outside the sport, and my mindset has always been that my fellow cyclists are colleagues rather than friends. Tiffany (along with Joanna Rowsell) is the exception to that. She's almost the same age as me, six months older to be exact, but I behave more like her big sister. We first met on our bikes; I'd raced against her so I knew her already. We didn't click immediately, to be honest. It took a little while, but she became a good friend. When we both became single we relied on each other a little bit more.

Tiff would do anything for anyone. She is hugely generous with her time and energy, massively creative in the artistic sense. She designs her own clothing, she's constantly cooking up new recipes, writing blogs, taking photos. She trains very hard, really loves her cycling and has endless enthusiasm and enjoyment of life, which sometimes has a destructive effect on her bike riding, so I am constantly telling her to rest and recover. She is also an incredible cook; she has a passion for food and healthy eating, and one spin-off of that friendship is that my diet had improved. Now, we train together frequently when we are both at home in Monaco; that's mainly through the summer, because she is back in Australia over the winter.

I have other friends in Monaco, mostly in Fontvieille, which is the quieter end of town with more of a family feel. As with anywhere you move to, you end up bumping into people and building a life; it's something I wouldn't be afraid of doing in the future it's simply a matter of being brave enough to do it. It's one of the benefits of being on a professional cycling team where you start each year with new teammates, mostly speaking different languages. You have to learn to build relationships quickly. When I first moved in with Adam, we lived opposite Harry Gibbings and his wife Jen, who are very sociable and tend to be instrumental in connecting people; the Irish moto GP rider Eugene Laverty and his wife Pippa moved into the same building, and were neighbours there, and so were the Paul and Laura.

On the night I went to Ikea and bought the bits and pieces for my new apartment I had to go to Pippa's birthday party. I say I had to go; I was knackered from putting the Ikea furniture together, so I was within an ace of skiving out of it. But Pippa is 'Mrs Sociable' – she wouldn't miss anything I was organising – so I thought, 'I can't let Pip down on her birthday', and I dragged myself down to the local bar for drinks. Eugene and Pippa had been helping a fellow Irishman, Philip Deignan, move to Monaco a couple of months earlier, after Phil had joined Team Sky. Phil is five and a bit years old than me, and had been a pro since 2005, starting out with AG2R before Cervélo – he'd won a stage of the Vuelta for them, and finished in the top ten overall – and then riding for RadioShack and United Healthcare before moving to Sky at the end of 2013.

We'd been teammates at Cervélo – it was Phil who

remembered the encounter at the dessert buffet in the hotel, not me – and we'd bumped into each other a couple of times already in groups of friends. That night, however, we got talking; we sat for an hour in a corner, chatting away, with the others looking at us and thinking, 'Oh, something is happening over there.' At that point nothing of that kind was remotely in my thoughts, but we started seeing each other a little more through groups of friends, and finally I made the first move and invited him out on a date: we went for a smoothie.

We were both racing here, there and everywhere, so I was convinced that Phil was humouring me, simply being nice to me to cheer me up. At the end of June I had a terrible race at the British national championship in Abergavenny. I lost out on the title after racing too aggressively and using a little too much brawn rather than brain. Laura Trott won the title and I came in third. It was a race where my lack of patience cost me the title.

The Tour de France started in Yorkshire the following weekend; I had been asked to do some work with sponsors at Harewood House just outside Leeds – the point where the first stage was flagged off – and while I was there, a completely unexpected message came from Phil: *Seeing that you have had a frustrating national championships, do you fancy escaping to Ireland for the weekend?* It came totally out of the blue: I thought, 'Whoa, I didn't realise we were at the visiting parents stage.' My second thought was: 'Why not?' So after the Tour had gone through Leeds I dashed to the airport and caught the most nervous flight of my life to Belfast City; Phil picked me up and we went to stay in Letterkenny, his home town in Donegal. The next day, we went horse riding on the beach. He didn't know that I was petrified of horses, but for a guy who doesn't really do romance or planning, he had put some serious effort in. After that I was in, hook, line and sinker.

CHAPTER 11

ME, MYSELF AND MY COACH

I finished the world championship at Ponferrada in north-west Spain in September 2014 barely out of breath. That was bitterly disappointing, more frustrating than the fact that I finished only seventh. I had felt really good. I had had a good season, albeit one where I had finished second more often than I wanted. I was motivated. I was one of the favourites. The course was tough, with a technically demanding section between the two climbs that would make recovering hard. It felt like the best chance I had ever had to win the world title; I liked the course and I believed I could win it. Afterwards, I could only reflect that the race had been too easy. That's a ridiculous thing to say when you don't win, but that's how it was.

I had inspected the course with Boels-Dolmans in June, because the team time trial at the start of the world championship week was a big goal for them. For that, and a day or two after, we stayed in a beautiful little family-run hotel up in the hills outside the town, a nice 20-minute ride from the course. Danny brought his scooter for us to train behind, everything was taken care of – we had two soigneurs – and there was fresh food out of the garden. I joined the GB team as late as possible because they were staying an hour and a half away.

Race day got off to a bad start. The food in the hotel was terrible, and when I came down on the morning of the race all the breakfast had gone, which was annoying. At the Worlds, the women's road race is usually in the afternoon; my preference is to wake up as late as possible and then to have a big breakfast-type meal rather than an early lunch. The only thing that was left that morning was one kind of cereal, and my first thought was, 'I can't race the world championships on that. I need more food than this.' So for this one I waited for lunch, but that was sloppy pasta, so it was barely worth the trouble.

When it came down to it, the race itself was never hard enough either to split up the field, or at least to ensure that my rivals' legs were tired when the finish came; I didn't have a team to make it hard, although the British girls – a young group including a couple of mountain bike riders – did what they could, and I tried myself just before the bell.

I had expected a tactical race due to the fact that Marianne Vos was off her usual form; so often the rest of the field would base their race on her, but here no one knew what she would do. As a spectacle it must have been awful. Everyone seemed to be waiting for the sprint. I kept thinking, 'Come on, let's go.' Frustratingly, the race stayed mostly together until the final lap before the Italians opened up on the very last climb; I took over when Emma Johansson accelerated, and then rode hard until four of us had a gap: me, Marianne, Emma and Elisa Longo Borghini. Nobody would commit, and the race came back together at a kilometre to go, with a group of 11 of us contesting the sprint. Tactically I had put my eggs in one basket – a break or at least a small selection – and I struggled to recalibrate quickly for the sprint. I decided to go with Giorgia Bronzini because she has won two world road-race titles – in 2010 and 2011 – sprinting from a group, so at the end of a world road race she should have been a good wheel to follow. In the event Giorgia went nowhere, and I was massively disappointed.

What we ended up with was a winner from a new generation of women's cycling stars: Pauline Ferrand-Prévot of France, who was only 22. Pauline is an amazing all-rounder, who has already been world champion at mountain bike and cyclo-cross; she'd got the better of me that Spring at Flèche Wallonne. She's tenacious, a little terrier, and a PR dream: she has a large social media following and personal sponsors, unlike many of the top women in our sport. French people know who she is, so when I'm on my bike, people shout at me in the street: 'Pauline, Pauline…'

After the race I stayed at the Irish team hotel and it was a completely different atmosphere compared to Great Britain; it felt like a family, with people asking, 'What can we do for you? What do you want?' I couldn't help noticing the difference. With GB, it felt as if there was no team environment at all. When I was a junior, I got a certificate through the post to say I had been selected for the world championship; now, you find out through the Internet, you turn up at a world championship and there are 20 staff you have never met before. When we were going to the track Worlds, someone would stand up at the start of the week and say, 'Congratulations on your selection, good luck, and know that all of the team is behind you.' You would feel the camaraderie; it was great. Now, you come into the GB team, you have no idea who anyone is, you don't know who to ask for a massage or for water bottles, or where to get your kit from. You just get a room number.

Losing that spirit felt like a huge, huge mistake. If you can bring the team together it adds a lot of value to your performance – just to be introduced to people, to know who people are – but GB cycling don't really do that any more. I had brought it up with the management because I felt it was something that was really valuable. If you look at the Great Britain athletics team, they appoint an athlete as team representative at the start of a competition and the whole outfit rallies together. Cycling isn't like that.

I want to make this absolutely clear: I don't want to point the finger at British Cycling for the fact that I didn't win in Ponferrada. Too many people blame the set-up there if they don't make it, rather than saying, 'OK, I will make it on my own without them', they use British Cycling as an excuse. If there is one thing that my personal story shows over the years, it is that you don't necessarily need the support of British Cycling to make it as a cyclist. Their backing can be immensely valuable, but it is not the most important item on the list.

* * *

Talking of lists, I have always been organised. I find it puts my mind at rest if I know what is coming up and I know that I have planned for it. I enjoy planning holidays, and figuring out the countdown to a goal during the season, because that means I have got control of things. It's something that clearly comes from my mum; we are both the planning type. When I was young, during the summer holidays, we would have six weeks up on a sheet of paper in the kitchen with activities pencilled in for most days. The flipside of that is that I am not particularly good at being spontaneous; I wish I was better at living in the moment. Once I have achieved a goal I can sometimes feel a bit lost, because I've got to the end of my plan. Usually, it takes a few days of being on holiday before I manage to unwind and enjoy the break in routine. Phil has been good at encouraging me to enjoy things more; every victory is worth celebrating before embarking on the next plan.

To begin with, my forays into self-coaching consisted of sitting down with a pen and paper and working out what I would do in the next week, thinking about the next race and how I would prepare for it. Tim Harris still has a couple of the planners I put up on the back of my wardrobe door in his and Jos's house in Belgium in 2009 and 2010 – they are massive calendar grids drawn up by hand, with the races marked on them, with distance, place and time; the races are colour-coded: blue for major races, green for stage races, according to their importance. Nowadays, it's far more sophisticated: I'm very-goal oriented. I phase plan through the season, figure out how I need to target specific races and some of the preparation – course recons, working out where to stay and where to eat – is done months in advance.

It took me a while to begin using power cranks – I didn't get my first pair until I joined Boels-Dolmans after the London Olympics. I didn't really like them to begin with. I think that was just an anarchic-minded response to my years in the British track system; I liked to think I could just ride my bike and that would be enough. I did that for a couple of years, but since I met Phil I have taken analysing my power more seriously. Watching him analyse his own power files every day made me realise it was a worthwhile exercise so I now use them to monitor what I am doing in terms of training; I have found that when used in tandem with the comments section in Training Peaks – the online training record that many riders use – they are a really useful tool.

The way I view Training Peaks has changed. Early on, when I started with the power cranks, I thought it was ridiculous to spend time every day uploading your training record and writing up your feedback. That attitude now seems ridiculous to me: you are a professional, and working in that way is what it is all about. Now, I upload my training levels every day, and write comments about how I have been feeling in general, and physically. Danny has my password so he can enter the site to look at how I'm training and what I'm writing, but he rarely does, so filling in the comments section is more like talking to myself. Phil finds it hilarious. He will see me writing away and will say, 'Who are you writing that to?' I just answer 'Myself.' What those comments give me is a continuous evaluation of how I am physically and what I am doing, which I can refer back to.

For example, in 2015 I was feeling really sluggish and low in the run-up to the Alfredo Binda World Cup race; in 2016 I had very similar feelings at exactly the same time and was reassured by looking at the comments I had made the previous year. Phil also pointed out that when I was filling in the comments section on the race in 2015 I had failed to mention that I had won – another example of forgetting to celebrate a win. It was a bit of a struggle even to find it, until I realised that I hadn't even written down that I won the race, just that I had felt rubbish in the build-up. So I was in a position to analyse that, and I could see that I had the same physical feelings before the race 12 months earlier, but I could also tell myself that I need make more of an effort at being positive.

As an athlete you learn how to interpret what your body is telling you. Over the years, one key learning curve was listening to what people were telling me, and comparing it with what I actually felt, particularly through the periods of illness, where I was pushing my body while trying to recover or limit the damage. People would be telling me, 'It is only a stomach ulcer, you'll be fine in ten days.' I would say I have learnt the value of rest, part of which is learning about how you will have peaks and troughs in your training: you can't maintain your very best for very long, so you have to allow yourself to come down from top form before building up again.

What I realised during 2014 was that in the past I had been maintaining an average level of fitness rather than allowing myself to be better. Before 2014, I would rarely have a complete rest day, and as a result I was consistently average when it came to fitness. What you mean by a rest day matters. For some people it might mean a 'coffee' ride – a gentle run out to somewhere nice – but what I mean is a complete day off the bike, when you don't do anything at all. You shouldn't use your rest days to catch up on stuff; I just lie on my sofa. In exceptional circumstances I might treat myself to a shopping trip to maintain balance in my life, but a rest day is a complete day off. It is not the same for everyone, but I love rest, and benefit so much from it. That is something I have found hard to explain to my friends and family; they don't understand the concept of rest as I do, which is why I struggle going home and why being in Monaco, in the 'bubble', is good for me. The way I see it, cycling is my profession, and I have to be as disciplined about resting as I am in training.

Often, riders train when they need to rest; that can be for reassurance – 'just to see' if they are as fit as they should be – and some train so they can allow themselves to eat. I've been there, but now, even on a rest day I maintain a good rhythm in my diet; I eat properly; I don't starve myself. Through the years of road racing, my body composition has changed since I gave up the track. I was about 60 kilos when I was a track rider, although I was always one of the smaller ones. Now, I am about 56 kilos at race weight: I am leaner, and I have shed a lot of fat. So I am carrying more muscle and have probably got rid of five or six kilos of unproductive fat.

One reason that I have managed to be consistent in the last two years is that I have not been ill, not properly, and I would put that down to my nutrition. Take my iron level; it is always something that I have to manage, like most female athletes. It can be made worse by the fact that I am a vegetarian; I have been ever since my parents allowed it. There is a good reason for it: when I was young I was determined that I wouldn't eat dead animals. It wasn't because I am an animal lover; I am actually scared of most animals, especially dogs. If you are a vegetarian and an athlete, you make it harder for yourself, but I never used to worry about my protein or iron intake at all – I never really understood the importance of it – so my levels used to be very low. I was frequently anaemic and I couldn't really control it.

I've learnt from various people over the years. At Garmin-Cervélo in 2011, I had an Italian teammate, Noemi Cantele, who had a very holistic approach to her training and diet. She was very much in touch with her body – rested when she was tired, ate all the right things and never starved herself. She was a really good influence; I learnt a lot from her. Tiffany Cromwell was helpful too, as she is an incredible cook, but in 2014 before I got together with Phil I was still doing things wrong. I was trying to be smaller, skipping my lunch, things like that.

The big change came when Phil moved in with me. That was when I started eating properly. He has been very important in that whole process of getting my diet right, having been a professional for a long time; he used to do stupid things as well – having grated carrot for tea and silly stuff like that – and it cost him dearly. He would see what I was doing and advise me to do things differently, not because he's worried about my cycling performance but because he cares about my general health. He would never let me miss a meal, never; he always tells me to eat more. He cooks properly, so he makes our protein porridge in the morning, and I do the dinner in the evening. He will remind me to have protein, just guide me subtly by asking me where it was – I don't know if it was conscious on his part or not, but that aspect improved. Since he started living with me, I probably eat twice as much as I used to. We often joke that it's the Irish Mammy in him.

Diet is about keeping consistency and rhythm in what you eat and when you eat it. In the past, I would manage my weight by eating badly, then not eating much, then eating badly again. I didn't understand nutrition at all. Now, I understand it and I am a believer in it, big time. At one point, I believed that 'nutrition' just meant health food. I thought that whether you were getting calories from a chocolate bar or a banana made no difference because the calories were all the same, so what was the problem? I now realise that what matters is the quality of what you eat: my grocery basket is more expensive, but I eat the best I can find. On average, I probably put away nine or ten pieces of fruit and vegetables a day: protein porridge with an apple and berries for breakfast, an omelette with salad, maybe three kinds of vegetables for lunch, and an evening meal of four different kinds of vegetables and perhaps a piece of fish. As a kid you learn about having 'five a day' – but I would never have imagined actually eating five items of fruit and veg a day.

Both male and female athletes can have a tendency towards food disorders such as bulimia and anorexia. I say 'a tendency', because in most cases it's not a matter of being unhealthily skinny in the anorexic sense, but of not being able to have a healthy relationship with food. This can include constantly talking about food, constantly feeling guilt about food, looking around at other people's plates to see what they are eating. In the track-racing environment weight wasn't an issue and the attitude was that food is just fuel, so the more you eat the better, but when you go into a women's professional road team, you are told, 'You can't eat this', you are asked, 'What's that you're eating?' If you were vulnerable you could end up in a dark place.

I can have a pretty level-headed attitude towards food but I have gone the other way as well. There were times when I used to binge, which I think is pretty normal, but it would prey on my mind when I was going into a race that, for example, I had overeaten the previous Tuesday when I really shouldn't have. When I was living on my own, I would come in from long rides and think that the best way to lose weight was to have an apple for my lunch and be hungry up until dinnertime, and then eat.

Now, although I might find it easier to slip back into bad habits when Phil is away and I am only cooking for myself, I always eat three meals a day. I never skip a meal and I have protein with every meal; I spend more on my groceries than I used to, and I prepare food properly. Whenever I go shopping I am thinking about my next three days' training and what food I will need to fuel those three days. It helps that I am cooking for Phil as well; an added motivation is that I want his meals to be good, too.

Eating more in order to lose weight sounds counter-intuitive, but that is how it seems to work. There are periods when I have to be very strict, six-week spells when I will not allow myself desserts or extra pieces here and there, but I have to be realistic: I am not a skinny climber but a powerful athlete. I need to give my body a chance. It's about working with your metabolism, giving your body a rhythm. That is something people don't understand: I've seen it so often – people eating badly, feeling bad about it, going to races feeling overweight although they have trained hard, and giving themselves a hard time. They are just making things more difficult for themselves. There is an element of self-knowledge, but it is also about understanding your body. There are days when you are irrationally hungry, but I listen and eat on those days: it is probably because my body requires extra food for recovery.

In terms of actual training, the biggest change is that I train to race now, rather than using racing as a way of getting fit. Sometimes, as a rider, when you don't permit yourself to dream of winning, it's an excuse you use, particularly when you are starting out. You are preparing yourself for failure; you go to a race and say, 'I'm doing this as training', and at the team meeting you might say,

'I'm here to do a job' rather than putting yourself out there and saying, 'I want to win. Can you all work for me?' That was something I found very difficult in 2013, when I wasn't particularly healthy. I was on a big team, and I was the best rider, so I felt responsible for trying to win at almost every race. Being able to stand up and say you want to win is something you have to grow into.

As a result, I race less often than before, and there are times when I push myself harder in training than when I race. I used to have the opposite problem: I wasn't able to train on my own because I didn't have the discipline I needed to do it. In that situation you end up thinking, 'Well, if I have to go to a race, that's free training and it will get me fitter.' That is something I have managed to eliminate; it's counter-productive because the travelling involved makes you tired, meaning you can't train.

I rarely train with Phil, but there are good reasons for that. I want to go out and do specific sessions, so does he. Additionally, it's important for our relationship to separate work and our off-the-bike life as far as we can; cycling is so overwhelmingly part of who we are that if we rode together as well as living together it would probably be too much.

Would I coach others? I'm not convinced I have the patience for it. I think I would be able to look at what other riders do and break it down for them, then advise them; I'm constantly looking at my teammates and wondering what they are not getting right. The most common mistake that most other riders make, in my view, is that they tend to over-train. They are not specific enough in their training, and they end up getting in too many 'junk miles'. Whether I would be able to work with other people is the question: the relationships between athlete and coach is key and it only works with trust. You really need to trust the advice you are being given and follow it completely rather than asking too many people and doing everything at 50 per cent.

Much of what I have ended up doing as my own coach is what most riders achieve with the help of a second party, but I see coaching myself as being about self-reliance. Some riders, like Phil for instance, flourish by working alongside a coach. I find it like an added layer of work that I can do without the complication of a second party. I was brought up to be independent; you don't ask for help unless you need it. I do really value those mentors who give me support when required – Westy, Phil and Danny – but my self-coaching is about taking responsibility for my own life and my own welfare. No one is going to provide me with a successful career or a shortcut to victory: I am going to find it for myself, and the way to find it is to constantly be the best version of myself that I can manage.

* * *

I found the disappointment of Ponferrada hard to get over. For most of the off-season, I couldn't switch off. I didn't take a long enough break from the bike; I was still in the gym every morning when Phil and I went on holiday. I just kept training harder, and didn't want to stop. It wasn't until about Christmas that I finally lost motivation just a little bit, or at least enough to take a step back and ask myself what I was doing. It was really eating me up, but there were lessons to be learnt. The most important thing was this: I had to realise that things don't always go to plan tactically, but I could at least have the confidence of knowing that I was one of the best in the world.

Another lesson was that I had to take all the variables out of the equation by being as prepared as I possibly could be. I wasn't going to rely on anyone to have breakfast ready for me in the morning; in future I would take my own breakfast box with me to ensure I had the things I needed. That's crucial, because if you let something unexpected like a poor breakfast get to you, you can throw away a year's work just like that. So I decided that at the 2015 world championship in Richmond, Virginia, I wouldn't eat in the team hotel if the food wasn't good enough. I would go out every night to a restaurant if need be, rather than have poor food irritating me and interfering with my preparation.

When I analysed the race at Ponferrada, it became clear that I had gone there in the best possible physical shape rather than planning and preparing specifically for a predetermined moment when I would attack. I went to Ponferrada prepared to race rather than ready to attack. Next time round, I wouldn't wait for what happened in the race to hamper me. So for the Worlds in Richmond in 2015, I would look really closely at the course and figure out exactly where I could win it. Working back from that I would need to make sure that the precise elements of fitness I needed would be in place on the day, depending on the course and the move I wanted to make, on precisely where I would attack to win. That meant, for three months in 2015, finishing a few training sessions each week with three 30-second efforts followed by a sprint. And so that I would know the difference between doing that effort in training and doing it with the fatigue of a world-class race in my legs, I would practise it in late August at the Grand Prix de Plouay, the final round of the World Cup before the road Worlds.

I also realised that going into Ponferrada, I had not had the winning feeling, thanks to that long run of second places. I needed the validation of winning at least one race in order to prove to myself that what I was doing in training was right. It was partly a matter of proving to myself that putting in those 30-second efforts followed by a sprint was the right thing to do, but I also needed to go through the pressure of wanting to win and delivering, rather than avoiding the expectation and hoping that I could put it together on the day. It was vital to go through that because having that level of responsibility isn't easy to deal with: telling your team that you are going to win, asking them to work for you, and then having to deliver it. To ensure I had that confidence before I travelled to Richmond I would have to win at Plouay, where I knew that the final part of the course was similar to that at the Worlds. Amid the disappointment and frustration, Ponferrada had told me that physically I could win the world road title, but in hindsight, in 2014 that race had probably come one year too soon.

CHAPTER 12

CATCHING RAINBOWS

Everyone in the room had their heads down. Well, almost everyone. Danny Stam didn't because he'd just torn a strip off the entire team; as for me, I rarely get upset after a bike race. On this occasion I probably should have been in tears because I had just missed out on a good chance to win the Tour of Flanders, one of my biggest goals. The Classic had been a disaster for Boels-Dolmans and this was the very frank post-race debrief. So heads were down; whether it was tears of frustration or riders being disappointed in themselves, in this room was the full range of post-race unhappiness.

Part of the reason for the bitter disappointment in 2015 was that the 2014 race had been flawless for us. When Ellen van Dijk won that year, with me taking second, I had been in seriously good shape – as was Ellen – and our tactic was that she would attack, and if that didn't work I would go. Her attack worked, which blocked me, but I was happy to finish second, obviously. I probably assumed that the following year I would have Ellen's support, but that didn't happen on the day. The plan was that everyone would look after me, but at the crucial moment when Elisa Longo Borghini made her move with about 20 kilometres to go, it was the responsibility of one of my teammates to close her down. They hesitated, and didn't do their jobs effectively, so I lost out. We all lost out.

I wasn't going to cry about it though. In moments like this – apart from two very exceptional occasions I've mentioned – defeat gives me renewed perspective. I was desperately disappointed. I was angry. It took me a while to get over it. However, we are all adults; I don't believe you should cry about failing to win a bike race. It's not so much that I see it as a weakness more that we are professionals rather than friends. I saw the debrief as a work meeting rather than as a place where you should let emotion take over.

However, going through this experience in Flanders was helpful when it came to planning my campaign to take the gold medal at the world road-race championships five months later. It backed up what I had felt after the immense disappointment at Ponferrada the previous September: I didn't want to be behind the moves. I wasn't going to end up on the back foot, reacting to other riders' attacks. I didn't care if people watching the race on television might think I was doing too much work, jumping on too many breaks. That wasn't going to bother me, because by now I knew that physically I was much better than the opposition. I was determined not to let the race get away from me in Richmond.

The build-up to the Worlds began during the week of the Philadelphia World Cup in early June. Before we travelled to Philadelphia, Danny and I drove to Richmond together to look over the TTT course for the team and the road course. He was in the car and I was on my bike, riding against traffic, getting lost in downtown Richmond. Somehow we had to find each other, and then make sure that we had both had a look at the correct roads. It was a typical Danny and Lizzie day out; we both ran out of roaming credit on our phones, so finding each other in downtown Richmond was a challenge.

Several things became clear to me. My sprint needed to be strong, and I needed form good enough to race hard over three consecutive climbs before the final sprint. On the first cobbled climb, Libby Hill, it would be important to be well positioned; if you weren't towards the front of the peloton you would spend the next ten kilometres fighting your way to the front again; you would be constantly on the back foot. So if you watch footage of the race, you will see that going into that climb I was never out of the top ten, usually in the top five – in every lap.

Next came a quick descent to the foot of the next cobbled climb, 23rd Street, the steep one where Peter Sagan was to make his winning attack in the elite men's race. You descended from that one, turned right, and then began the final drag: Governor Street. A left turn, and then there were about 550 metres left to the finish line, still a relatively long way to go. I studied the wind every day; there always seemed to be a headwind on the finishing straight. I didn't want to end up in a position where I attacked up Governor Street and was pushing into a block headwind on the home straight with the peloton on my heels. So the idea I came up with was that my last attack up Governor Street would be at 85 per cent, rather than 100 per cent, so I would have something left in the tank for the sprint.

That was the plan: it would mean I wouldn't end up on my own, and I would have to win the sprint from what I hoped would be a reduced lead group. I decided that I would then take the rest of the leaders up to the left-hand side of the road so that I could prevent them from attacking up that side: any attack that was going to come would be on the right. The road surface was off-camber – it sloped downwards slightly to the right – so that if anyone did attack I could use the camber falling away from me to gain momentum, as I would on a velodrome.

I also sorted out where and what I would eat if the food in

the hotel was not good enough. We checked out the Boels-Dolmans hotel – where we would stay for the team time trial – but being in America there was an even chance that the food in the Great Britain hotel wouldn't be good. That is where Wholefoods Market came in – it's a fancy organic supermarket chain, which is fairly expensive but which sells ready-made fresh salads and other food. I located one of those and made sure I knew where another good restaurant was. As it turned out, I had only one meal in the hotel; the food was terrible, so that was that.

I also thought about equipment. I would have to talk to our sponsors Zipp about what kind of wheels to use because of the need to have a stable ride over the cobbles. Tyre type and pressure would be critical for adhesion, and that might well change depending on the chance of rain. As far as the Great Britain team that would be racing with me was concerned, I had no input. That didn't matter, because – I appreciate that this sounds arrogant, but this is how it was – no matter what team they selected there wouldn't be anyone to help me at the finish.

As for training, I needed to be powerful. I wanted to be completely ready for that particular course. In Ponferrada I had been generally fit but here I didn't want to be the fittest in the race. I wanted to win it. Taking it backwards, I had scheduled in a trip to Rio in August to look at the Olympic road-race course – it wasn't ideal but it was important – so I had to work around that. July was going to be overload volume, August was power and September would be race and then freshen up.

If you think about form as a cake, it's a little easier to understand how much of each ingredient you need and where to start. The flour and the eggs are your volume: long steady miles and strength work on the bike or in the gym that effectively works on your overall fitness so that you have overall condition to cope with the intervals that come later. Your icing is your power, where you start to bring in shorter intervals: you turn the strength and fitness you have gained into power by essentially adding speed into your training. The cherry is my favourite phase, where most of the volume goes from your training to be replaced by racing and recovering.

* * *

There was just one hiccup and it came in the Tour of Britain, not long after we returned from the US recce. When the race entered the Suffolk coastal town of Aldeburgh in one long high-speed string, I went over the line first by a mile, delighted, hands in the air. Then it went wrong. The finish was on the coast road, with the sea on the left. After the line the road bent slightly to the right so the curve took us that way as well; the line of press and photographers standing just beyond the line were slightly to the left too. My hands were in the air, a gust of wind took my front wheel away; straight away I came down to grab the bars. I could still save myself by pulling the bike to the right, but the wind just pulled me to the left. There wasn't enough distance before the row of photographers, standing 40 metres after the finish.

I barrelled into them and then there was absolute carnage. There was one photographer, Huw Williams, kneeling down with a camera; I hit him with my front wheel on the side of his head. His ear was black afterwards. I piled into the race organiser as well, into his shoulder, but it was Huw who took the first impact. I always get up straight away. Whenever I fall off my bike I jump up no matter where I land, but this time I was in too much shock. I landed directly on my leg; you can see from the video of the stage finish how much of the impact is on my femur and my hip. My leg just went dead. I was sure it was broken. My first reaction on the floor was, 'Have I killed that guy I've just hit?' I was petrified. 'How is he? How is he?'

In the meantime my left leg had gone into spasm and completely locked up, and when my team manager Danny arrived on the scene, I had to ask him if the bone was sticking out. That's how much it hurt. Straight away I was certain my season was over. I was lying there thinking that 2015 was gone but I might be OK for the Rio Olympics, so I didn't think at all about the pain I was suffering.

The ambulance was there almost at once. My helmet was smashed up so they carefully put on a neck brace and placed me on a spinal board. I was in shock and in a lot of pain, and remained that way for half an hour or more while they worked out what I had done and while they cut my shoes off because of the swelling.

When they got me ready to go to the hospital, there was one thing I didn't want to happen: 'Don't you dare put me in that helicopter.' I don't trust helicopters – too risky for me. I refused to get into it, so they put me out; apparently Danny had a quiet word with the medics and they put me to sleep. I remember a guy in an orange suit telling me to focus on nice things. So I began thinking of holidays, and I have vivid memories of the sea, where there were waves of coconuts and palm trees.

When I woke up, I was in the ward. I found out that the doctor treating me was a triathlete, which was a relief. It is always lucky if you end up with medical staff who are into sport because they give you the relevant care for your discipline – it's not a matter of getting special treatment, more that as they themselves are athletes they understand how to help get you back on your bike again as soon as possible. After all the tests, it turned out that all that was wrong was an extreme dead leg as if I'd been thumped; I also had a haematoma on my thigh, a sprained wrist and had received a blow to the head, although I hadn't lost consciousness. That was all. So I checked myself out, made sure I had a couple of easy days and then began to figure out how I was going to get back for the national championships. I was in good form, and I wanted to make use of it.

*   *   *

I had already decided I would need to win at the GP Plouay at the end of August for my confidence, and to test attacking and sprinting in quick succession. That went perfectly as I had hoped, which was not a surprise but a massive confidence boost nonetheless. My parents came to watch and Phil was racing the next day in the men's race. Unusually Phil was able to watch the full race on TV in his hotel, as was my sister via livestream at home. My confidence was boosted further by their analysis of how dominant I was; they didn't realise 'how good I was'.

I went to stay with Mum and Dad at their campsite in Plouay for the night before staying to watch Phil. Lying in the caravan I remember feeling quite amused at my situation. I had just won the World Cup for the second year in a row and here I was celebrating on a campsite with my parents sleeping in the bed I had spent so many holidays in as a child. I couldn't help thinking even if there was parity in our sport, and my recent success had earned me millions, I wouldn't have wanted to be anywhere else. Phil told me later that he had planned to ask my dad for my hand in marriage that weekend, except he couldn't get a word in edgeways with me and my mum always around.

*   *   *

World championship week began with the team time trial on the Sunday six days before the road race. Boels-Dolmans finished second, just six seconds behind the winners; I was one of the strongest in the team, which pushed my confidence up again. At that point I knew I was physically and mentally ready. Not that the team hotel was an easy place to be. You spend a week with your teammates, and their way of dealing with pressure is different to mine, which made it uncomfortable. There wasn't much chat at the dinner table. Everyone was stressed out, a bit neurotic. It was like treading on eggshells, and the different time zone made it difficult to call home and have a normal chat with someone.

After the team time trial all the other riders moved to their national team hotels, but I wanted to join Great Britain as late as possible. In the few days I stayed on with Boels-Dolmans, I had another good look at the three climbs that would close the road race, and replicated exactly what I had been doing in training: I attacked each climb hard, and then sprinted for the finish.

I moved into the GB hotel on the Thursday. The team had wanted me to do a ride with the other girls that day because the roads were closed for the road races – it's the usual thing to do as you can look at the course – but I never go on that day because it doesn't fit in with how I schedule my rest day, which is the Thursday before the race. On the day before the race, I usually ride for an hour and a half with three sprints to activate my body. Some people might say that it is important to ride with the girls to bond with them, so that you've at least done a training ride before you race together, but I wasn't going to compromise my preparation. I wasn't there to ride around.

I was sharing with Jessie Walker, who is also from Yorkshire like her father Chris. She was one of several young girls on the team who were lovely to be with: all new to it, all excited, all enthusiastic and keen to do the best job that they could. They were all nervous about letting me down. They were the best side to the few days I spent with GB in Richmond, but collectively, they made me feel very old. I was keen to work with them as they were a lovely group, so over the days I spent with GB I put some time and effort into sitting and talking with them, trying to make sure that we felt like a team.

The next day, the GB team manager, Brian Stephens, asked to sit down with me to talk about the race. I told him my plan; his view was that I should wait for the sprint.

'Did you watch Plouay?'

'I saw photos.'

The person who was responsible for choosing the women's road-race team hadn't even watched highlights of the last World Cup; he wanted to base my strategy on photographs. At that point, I switched in my mind: 'Lizzie, why are you opening yourself up to advice and input from a stranger when they haven't had any input all season? Go back into your bubble and ignore it.'

I had had a brief catch-up with the then British Cycling technical director Shane Sutton in the winter of 2015 and he said he wanted me to try Brian as my coach. I thought I would try to give it a go, because in the position I'm in it is important for me to have a relationship with British Cycling and in a way they were offering to help me. So I wasn't going to say no. I met Brian; he is a nice guy, but the six-week programme he suggested to me didn't have a single rest day in it. His proposed rest day was one where I rode 'easy'; I need actual rest. That is not to say that he is not a good coach – he coaches professional men such as Michael Matthews very successfully – but I could immediately see that we were on a different wavelength and had different approaches. It wasn't going to work for me.

We had the team meeting; we told Brian exactly what we needed to eat on the morning of the race. I then sat with Brian and told him exactly what wheels and tyre pressures I wanted according to the weather conditions. Depending on whether or not it was raining, the implications would be massive over the cobbles. You want to have the pressure just right so that the tyres don't jump going uphill and don't slide going down. I repeated it over and over again: it was vitally important to me if I was going to make those efforts over those climbs at the decisive moment in the race.

Race morning came and the food we had asked for wasn't there. We had been clear that we needed rice and eggs and what we were given was a big drum of overcooked pasta.

There didn't seem to be a single member of the hotel staff who we could ask to speak to the restaurant staff to sort it out. I tried to explain to one of the waiters just how important it was: this is a world championship, we have worked for months for this, and we need to get these things right. But his answer was that the kitchen was closed and there was nothing he could do. Luckily I had made sure I had my own breakfast with me and was self-sufficient.

We got our bikes ready to ride to the start and Jessie asked, 'Lizzie, should we get race food and drinks here?'

'Don't worry, that will all be up at the course; there will be soigneurs, bottles, all that stuff.'

We had discussed with the team management that we wouldn't go and sit in the team's camper van before the start; we would get ready in the pits, which were in a sports hall. We got there, and it was empty. We went to the camper and it was locked. There was an hour to go to race time and I was getting thirsty. I had no idea what was going on. I couldn't find a single staff member anywhere. I had understood that Brian would be there; there would be a mechanic, a soigneur as per normal. But there was not a member of staff to be seen.

Luckily I had my phone. I called Abby Burton, the GB press officer, and said, 'Abby, if this isn't sorted out within ten minutes I will not be able to hold myself back from telling the media about it at the end of the race. This needs to be fixed and fast.' Abby managed to get hold of the team doctor. It turned out that Brian was the junior men's coach as well as looking after us and was actually in the team car following the junior men's race, as was our mechanic.

There were clouds and rain – on and off – I had no idea what pressure had been put in my tyres, I still hadn't had a drink, and still no one was around. Eventually one of the soigneurs, Luc, turned up; he was meant to be looking after the junior men after their race, but said he would sort us out. He got us up to the race route and found us drinks and so on.

I then called Danny: 'I've no idea what wheels are in the bike or what pressure is in the tyres. Please, can you come and sort it out?'

'Lizzie, I'm at the other side of the course.'

'Please, can you run? Now.'

Eventually, Danny arrived and borrowed a pump from the Swiss team and got my tyres to the pressure that was needed. Apparently the British mechanic hadn't been told, although it was something that I had been adamant about.

Danny calmed me down and I went to sign on. I actually went to the toilet and burst into tears. I was so upset. It was the contrast in the level of support between the men's and the women's teams that got me. I knew I was the favourite to win the race. I knew what Mark Cavendish had had going into the 2011 world championship – chefs at the hotel, everything he could possibly have wanted – and there I was stuck outside the camper van without a key thinking, 'I'm thirsty, what is going on here?' I had thought I had controlled everything I could, and GB would at least get race day right.

It was cathartic, getting that pent-up energy out, and the girls around me were great; they handled me quite well and were very calming. It can't have been easy for them, given how young they are, to see their team leader in that position and not be sure what on earth they could do to fix it. Once I had burst into tears, I actually felt quite relaxed.

* * *

I get bored quite easily during races. I flourish in a hard race where I have to react physically. The problem in a race like the Worlds is that I know the final two laps are what really matters, so I have to get through the period up to then as patiently as possible. I do it by focusing on the simple things. I make sure my placing is right, that I am always at the front of the peloton. Sometimes people criticise me for this – they say I stay too close to the front, not hiding in the wheels to save energy – but I find it easier that way. I concentrate on eating and drinking and spinning, going up the climbs in as low a gear as possible, staying in the saddle to put as little strain on the legs as I can. One peculiarity of the Worlds is that you go through the finish several times, so I keep looking at it, checking where the wind is from, how strong it is and always checking the markers I've set down in my mind. I never look at the little signs saying 'one kilometre to go' and so on, I look at big, obvious things such as where the grandstand starts or a zebra crossing. Here, the crossing was at 400m to go, the grandstand at 250.

The team had a whiteboard in the feeding zone. Every lap it told me another teammate had gone: Jessie out, Molly Weaver out, Lucy Garner gone, and with three laps to go it said: 'Lizzie, game on.' Then, I knew I was on my own. An attack had gone away – a group of nine – but I knew every rider in the group and I wasn't worried. There were some decent riders in there and some good nations – Italy, Australia, Netherlands, Germany, every big nation – but the gap was never huge and I knew they were all second-tier riders. It was the Dutch who started chasing – clearly they weren't confident in the chances of Amy Pieters, who was in the move for them – so I settled in behind them.

When we hit 23rd Street for the second-last time, I did put a little dig in. I thought, 'I just need to bring this back a little, just enough to give the chasers a bit of hope.' So I pulled it back a few seconds, so that the leaders would start to give up slightly, and the chasers would get a fraction more motivation. And it opened up my legs, put some tension in the muscles. It was a dummy – and that felt great, because I could see other riders under pressure and getting dropped. You think, 'Well, if you are getting dropped now, before the last lap…'

At a lap to go, we began to see the nine ahead of us, on the long straight stretch before we turned right on to the cobbles; we caught them going into the succession of climbs. It was Trixi Worrack, the German, who led out up Libby Hill for the last time; we opened a small gap, with a few more riders just behind, and at that point I would have loved to have just gone for it. Instead, I had to tell myself, 'Patience, patience. If this all comes back you will have to rely on your sprint, so don't burn all the matches too early.' On the next one, the Polish girl, Kasia Niewiadoma, attacked, and again I went with the move; again we opened up a few metres' lead, but no one was willing to commit. Again, I had to tell myself, 'Right, let them come back; let them come back. If they are getting dropped now, they will be working hard behind to catch up. Stick to the plan. Stick to the plan.'

On the downhill off 23rd Street, it was Tiffany Cromwell who attacked. It was too easy just to roll on to her wheel. She's my good friend and training partner; for a split second that crossed my mind, but I wasn't prepared to give it away. 'I am not letting this move go. She is an underdog and they won't follow her; they will all look at me, so I can't let her go.' You have to be ruthless in those moments. I knew I had worked the hardest and made the most sacrifices: 'This race is mine.'

When we started Governor Street, Lucinda Brand of Holland was the first to attack; it wasn't hard to bring her back because of the momentum in the group with everyone fighting for position. One thing Danny had said to me earlier was, 'Attack from behind. Go from behind.' At that late stage of the race I had to find the confidence to drop right back in the group. I actually had to put the brakes on so that I would be far enough behind to come past the front-runners with enough speed that they would have no chance of getting near my wheel.

I went to the back, changed up to the big chain ring, and went for it. I don't think they were expecting it; the normal thing to do at that stage would be to wait for the sprint rather than risk wearing yourself out. But it was the key attack of the race, because the reaction as they chased me shook out anyone who was tired; there were only eight of them left, although at that stage I wasn't counting. Once they had caught me, I took them to the left side of the road; no one would take a turn, but instead of letting that frustrate me as it would have in previous years, I did exactly what I had done in Plouay: kept up the speed so that no one could take me by surprise, and kept the left-hand side closed. I needed that clear run to the line and I wasn't going to leave it to chance.

I knew I would win before the sprint started, when the other eight riders left me on the front. I knew that if you were in that group with me you had to pre-empt me. I knew none of them were faster than me; I knew I would be faster than any of them whether I started from the front or the back. Effectively, I was with a group of climbers – not pure climbers, but I had dropped all the best sprinters. Their best chance of winning was to attack me just before the sprint but nobody did that, which meant they had nothing in their legs. They were waiting for me, which was what I needed: I wanted to dictate it; that was my strength.

I knew roughly where we were because we had arrived at the grandstands. I was thinking, 'Ooh, they are leaving it late here.' If no one else started that sprint, it would be down to me, but Anna van der Breggen went first. And that was it: I was not going to be stopped. I hadn't put my hands in the air when winning races since the crash that June; it was something that still went through my mind. Hands on the bars, then hands over my mouth; not the most elegant winning salute. I wasn't exactly in shock, but thinking, 'Shit, I have done it. Oh shit. I am the World Champion.' It was pure delight.

* * *

Before Richmond, I had had the same thoughts as before Glasgow: I am not a champion. Even my name, Lizzie Armitstead, doesn't sound like the name of a champion. 'It's not quite Usain Bolt,' I thought; it sounds like what you would call a silver medallist. Winning in Glasgow was important, but I said to myself, 'It's only the Commonwealth Games, not against the whole world.' As I did the reconnaissance and all the other work in the run-up to Richmond, I couldn't keep that doubt away: I would be in the best shape possible but there would always be something that would stop me winning gold.

The feeling of relief once the rainbow jersey was on my back was almost physical. I felt as if I could finally stand up straight. It was as if I'd been to the physio had a back massage, and had all the tension taken out of my spine. Trying to reach a goal on that scale consumes you without your being aware of it, so when it finally happens, you feel a massive release from all the strain, from constantly having that single thing on your mind.

That evening, the girls and I got together, got dressed and went downstairs: Shane gave the entire team champagne to toast me, which was unexpected, and nice. We didn't eat dinner – the food was still terrible – so out we went. I took the British girls to the bar where Evelyn Stevens – a top American rider who was my teammate at Boels-Dolmans – was having her bachelorette party, and at that point, due to haste and overexcitement, I made a mistake. Throughout the year I had been talking to Evelyn about the fact that I had never tasted tequila; she thought it was incredible that I had reached 27 and never tried it. So I ordered tequila for all my friends, but unfortunately I miscounted; I thought there were 25 of us, but in fact we were only half a dozen.

My miscalculation meant the GB team peaked too early, and we were all in a taxi by about 11:30pm. It was a short but fun night, at the end of which I had to put one or two of my younger teammates to bed. Unfortunately, the following morning we had a photo shoot for British Cycling at 9am; Lucy Garner was still in a bad way, but we managed to get her up to the top of the roof for the pictures, she managed to smile and then she crawled back into bed. It all made me feel even older than before; it was refreshing to be with a group of girls who were genuinely very happy for me, to be with people who saw what I had done as such a big deal. But it was hard at the same time, because I really wanted to be at home.

After the Worlds, I had trouble stopping. Phil and I had become engaged on his birthday, 7 September, but we had not had a single moment to savour it. The following morning he had left for Ireland to be with his parents. I felt very lucky to be marrying into the Deignan family; they are wonderful people and Donegal is a beautiful place. I flew straight from Richmond to Ireland and although we only had a few days there before I had to go to the Netherlands again, it was a special few days.

The next stop was the Netherlands for the team's sponsorship day, which is an 80-kilometre ride with all the sponsors taking in various cafe stops. It is a hard day at the office, physically because the sponsors all want to show off, and mentally because as a team it is the end of the season and we have just spent two weeks cooped up together in a hotel for the world team time-trial championship, all under pressure; we aren't that keen to see each other again.

I am a holidays person; a planner, I love to look forward to my breaks, to think about them, but there wasn't much chance. It was a similar feeling to post-2012: all I wanted to do was see my family and friends and enjoy the reward for all my hard work, but in reality that's never possible in the immediate aftermath of a world title. My absolute priority was to spend time with my new fiancé and his family. We didn't know what we were going to do because we didn't want to be too far from Ireland under the circumstances, and that meant we didn't want to go too far away, or for too long. My grandparents were having their diamond wedding anniversary at the same time; we were pulled in so many different directions. We managed a five-day break in Sicily, but it wasn't really long enough; there was never a period of just being together and relaxing completely. Phil's pre-season bonding session with Team Sky wasn't far away, and there were opportunities for me that I couldn't turn down. It was a matter of trying to make the most of the time we had while thinking about 2016 and trying not to get too tired.

In October I decided to contact British Cycling to set up a meeting with Shane and Brian to analyse Richmond and discuss organisational support ahead of Rio. I arranged for the meeting to be in London at my agent's office so Emma could be there as I wanted her support. Considering how poor the support in Richmond had been, I went into the meeting prepared for a major confrontation, so I was a little taken aback when Shane held his hands up directly and apologised. He acknowledged that I had been let down in Richmond, but he didn't want to blame any individual person for it. Neither did I. The truth was the whole team was lacking structure and leadership. Individually everyone was doing their best.

We spent the rest of the meeting discussing how British Cycling could help me in the run-up to Rio. I explained the relationship I have with Danny and how important it was for me to have him in Rio. I also negotiated my own physio and travel schedules. As the women's road coach, Brian must have felt fairly pushed out at this meeting, so I am grateful for his understanding of the situation. It's common when you have a successful athlete for too many people to want a slice of the actio,n but Brian was respectful of my team and the process we wanted to put in place.

British Cycling is where I started my career. There have been moments in my career where I have felt that their support hasn't been good enough, but the truth is that the organisation is full of committed and talented individuals who have made essential contributions to my career. I believe the organisation is evolving in terms of its support for women on the road at under-23 level. This is where young women with talent need to be nurtured so that we have a big enough pool of elite athletes to require a full-time women's road coach.

CHAPTER 13

ALL ROADS
HAVE POTHOLES

On most training days, Phil and I follow a similar routine. Get up, put the porridge on, and have a big breakfast. People would be shocked by how much breakfast I get through. We have coffee, sit down and watch the television news – the BBC or Irish – while we let the breakfast go down, then it's kit on for between three and five hours' training. After I get back, I have lunch, sometimes a massage, maybe some stretching or core stability work, and then usually there is something to do: go to the bank, the supermarket or the post office. By the time I'm back it's dinnertime. After that I take to the sofa, perhaps FaceTime or call someone at home and look at emails and then go to sleep. Then I get up the next morning and do it all over again.

This doesn't sound exciting or glamorous but cycling as a profession leaves little room for much else. Absolutely everything I do has consequences for my performance. You can't think, 'I will go out and have a drink tonight', because that rolls on to the next day, which subsequently has an impact on the whole week's training. That in turn could make a difference in a race, which could affect your contract and your entire future. That bigger picture and constant need to think about the consequences of what you do sometimes becomes overwhelming and makes you contemplate retirement.

I love living in Monaco, and it's perfect for what I am trying to do as a cyclist, but I still miss a lot about life back home: my sister and her two children, my friends, fish and chips, Cheddar cheese. I miss normal life. My family always eats together every Sunday night, so I particularly miss them then.

Living in Monaco has had an immense impact on my cycling: the terrain means it's difficult to do a flat ride so you're always pressing hard on the pedals, even on recovery rides. That has made me perform better, and I get consistent training because of the sunshine all year round. People back home say that 'all that bad weather builds character', but this is a hard-enough job without getting ill because you're soaking wet and eating the dirt that sprays up off the road. But it is being in the bubble that helps most: at home I always have things to do – commitments to sponsors, commitments in the community, things you wouldn't expect. To succeed you have to say 'no'. You have to lock yourself away and I can do that here.

I loved wearing my world champion's jersey through 2016. I would wear it at every opportunity I could manage. I told interviewers that I would look at myself in shop windows as I rode past to remind myself that it was real.

Through spring and early summer I managed to string together a series of major wins: Het Nieuwsblad, Strade Bianche, the Binda Trophy, the Tour of Flanders, the Tour of Britain. It was a high 'hit rate' as a proportion of races ridden, about one in two, up to the end of June. That felt good: it's hard to win a single road race, let alone nearly half of the ones you ride. With the rainbow jersey on my back, I felt confident when I pinned a number on, and sure enough in myself to tell Boels-Dolmans which races I wanted to ride. Racing less often meant I was more rested and relaxed when I did compete; it was a virtuous circle.

The Tour of Flanders was the race I had always wanted to win ever since I started to learn about cycling. As a race, it has everything that I love about the sport: an iconic route, an incredible atmosphere on the course, the physical attributes that you need to win it. You have to be a great all-rounder; there are no lucky winners in Flanders. Bad weather, cobbles and the ferocious desire of every other woman in the race to win means it is so hard to take victory.

Boels-Dolmans dominated, as we had done since the

start of the season. Everyone had her role, and everyone committed and executed perfectly. Christine Majerus took care of me from the start, and did me proud. I was never out of position, and in the end the strength I saved made a huge difference. I barely felt the wind early on. Megan Guarnier forced a selection on the Kruisberg; 20 kilometres from the finish there were only about 20 of us at the foot of the Oude Kwaremont. Over the radio, we were told that Ellen van Dijk was to make the race hard as it was still too much together; my plan was to escape over the Paterberg, the final climb, and we needed a more aggressive race so that I could get away.

Ellen's pace on the Oude Kwaremont brought everyone to their knees. Emma Johansson attacked at the top, I accelerated with her; we had a small advantage heading for the final climb of the race the Paterberg. Emma decided to sit in my wheel rather than contribute to enhancing our lead, I had the confidence to think, 'This can still work. I'll attack her on the Paterberg.' I tried, but there was no way I could get her off my wheel. She decided to work a couple of kilometres after the top, and we worked together until the final kilometre.

It ended up with just two of us in front and the peloton on our heels; we had to commit. I wasn't able to hold anything back for the sprint as Emma had been sitting in my wheel from the 1km to go sign, Emma is fast – she has been one of the great all-rounders of women's cycling over the years – and

I didn't underestimate her. It was tight in the final kilometre; we could see the chasing group. Although I had three teammates in there to discourage the rest, I needed Emma to open up the sprint, and she did. At that point it's not about who is fastest, it comes down to who is more fresh. I was tired, and you could see that from my sprint; I had no kick at the beginning of my sprint and it was a real drag race to the line. My momentum took me over the top of her, so I knew in my gut I had won, but I didn't dare to risk celebrating. I only knew for certain I had won when she came and congratulated me. I had landed another race of my dreams.

Just like after the Worlds, straight away I felt lighter, the relief was instant, the pressure was off. The 2015 race had haunted me: it had been a massive goal, I'd worked all winter for it, I'd been in physical shape to win it, and it had eluded me. I had won the 2016 Tour of Flanders when I was tired, really tired; I had managed to pull it off in spite of that. To know I could still win one of the hardest races on the calendar even when I was tired, when the preparation hadn't gone perfectly, was a massive boost to my confidence. Those wins meant I had fulfilled my contract to Boels for 2016, I had represented my team well and I could ask for a certain amount of freedom to train on my own, rather than trying to keep winning more. I could finally shift my focus to Rio, because winning Flanders left me with one big goal: the Olympics.

* * *

With that succession of major victories, my life that winter and spring must have looked seamless to outsiders. But it wasn't that simple. The days I had spent with Phil in Sicily in October 2015 with the rainbow jersey in the bag should have been an idyllic holiday, but it was far from it. I usually cut myself off from the outside world when I'm on holiday, but I had a text from my dad: he had a letter from UK Sport; should he open it?

The letter from UKAD was to notify me of the second strike, given to me after a spot check on my whereabouts from the previous week, where my overnight accommodation and my morning time slot didn't correlate.

Here we should go into the system in detail. If you are an athlete in the out-of-competition testing pool, you have to provide two daily pieces of information through the database known as ADAMS (Anti-Doping Administration and Management System): a location and a time slot of one hour each day in which you are available for testing, and the address where you will be staying overnight. A missed test is when they come and knock on your door at the place where you have said you will be for that one-hour slot, and you are not there. A filing failure is when something in the details you have given doesn't add up – for example when your overnight accommodation doesn't match your morning time slot. It doesn't necessarily mean the testers have been to your front door – it may simply be someone checking in the computer and coming across a contradiction that you can't adequately explain.

You are effectively accountable for 24 hours a day. The system isn't simple: you have to provide complete information about where you are – hotels, flights, everything. For example, for a given day, I might say, 'Testing hour, Monaco, between six and seven in the morning.' If I were flying to Belgium that same afternoon, my next 'Testing hour' slot would be Belgium the following morning, but I would also have to provide details of which flight I would be catching and explain that I would be sleeping in Belgium in overnight accommodation; if they came to test me that evening, and I wasn't Where I had said I would be, the question would be asked: where is the proof that you stayed in the Belgium hotel? Previously, a 'random' test that is attempted out of your designated one-hour test slot would not need an explanation and would not result in a strike. Now you must be accountable at all times. There are various grey areas. One is how much notice you have to give before you change your overnight accommodation – there is no rule about that. For your time slot, you have up to a minute before it begins in which you can change it, but if you do that, it puts you in the 'suspicious' category.

I've given details of the first 'strike' already, but I take full responsibility for that second one. Off-season is probably the most difficult time for athletes to correctly update their whereabouts; you go from a life of discipline and routine to having the chance to 'live normally'. I was immensely busy, I had no idea where I was going to be day to day between visiting friends and family and fulfilling off-the-bike commitments, but ultimately it was down to me to get it right. The October 2015 strike was a 'filing failure'. It was an honest mistake. I told the Court of Arbitration in Sport in July 2016: 'For the night of 5 October 2015... ADAMS indicated that I was in Monaco, when I was actually in Leeds. This was brought to UKAD's attention because on the evening of 5 October I accurately updated my specified one-hour testing slot for the following day – 6 October – to reflect the fact that I was in Leeds. If I had not updated my whereabouts for 6 October in this way, then UKAD might never have known of the inaccurate filing for 5 October.'

In other words, it was my own accurate update that drew UKAD's attention to my mistake, and to my knowledge no one else has ever had this kind of retrospective failure. That didn't change the fact that the second strike put me on the brink of disaster. If I ended up with a third strike in the next ten months, I could well be out of the Olympic Games.

In December 2015, British Cycling gave me the chance to have a session with a representative of UK Sport so that I understood the changes and developments the ADAMS system had made. I had only ever had one chance to be educated about the formalities of the 'whereabouts' system since I first moved to Manchester ten years earlier and the system had evolved considerably since then, so it was obvious that I needed to be re-trained. To give one example, when I began doing 'whereabouts', there was no separation between overnight accommodation and the morning testing slot. At the meeting we agreed that Simon Thornton, British Cycling's compliance manager, would monitor my whereabouts on a weekly basis, so that if there was a discrepancy as in October he would notice and alert me. I had emails where I wrote to him 'just checking my whereabouts is OK as I haven't heard anything [from you] for a little while, just want to confirm that I am filling it in correctly.' I got a reply saying effectively, 'no news is good news'. So that was reassuring.

* * *

When the phone rang at 6am on 9 June it felt as if I was being violently punched in the stomach. The caller was a Doping Control Officer (DCO) waiting outside my apartment in Monaco; I was in bed in Ireland. I understood the implications immediately and I went into shock. Pure shock, just shaking uncontrollably, saying over and over again, 'No, no, no, this can't be possible, this can't be possible'. Phil was with me and held me as I shook and cried. I was absolutely certain that I had filled in my 'whereabouts' correctly; catastrophically, I hadn't. I will have to live with that burden as long as I race. It still haunts me. I still wake up in the night sweating and triple-checking my phone to be certain I haven't done it again.

I simply couldn't understand how it had happened, knowing what had been put in place for me. Since I got the second strike in October 2015, I had been so focused on it, so diligent. This was the one time I made a mistake.

Since I have known Phil his father Gerry had been suffering with terminal cancer, and we would spend as much time as our schedules allowed to be back in Ireland with Philip's family. Philip pulled out of the Giro d'Italia on Friday, 27 May 2016, two days before it was due to finish. He had been suffering with severe fatigue and couldn't continue. I had just won a race in the Netherlands and had flown home; after picking Phil up, at that last minute we decided to fly home to Ireland as soon as we could because of the unscheduled correlating gap in both of our schedules. I updated my whereabouts to Ireland from that day until the morning of a sponsorship day in Holland on 9 June, for which I had left my whereabouts as Monaco until I knew exactly where I was going to be. When I was in Ireland, I had to travel to Scotland for a day to do some sponsorship work; and on return I updated my whereabouts to Ireland, Ireland, Ireland, all the way through until I was due to go to the Aviva Women's Tour on 15 June. By now I'd agreed with my team manager that I could miss the sponsor day in Holland, because I needed to be in Ireland with Phil's family at this time as things had taken a turn for the worse. What I didn't realise was that I had not changed that single day in my whereabouts when

I should have been in Holland to Ireland; it had remained on my default address: Monaco.

I always check my whereabouts, every night for the next morning – I even have an alarm on my phone. I always do it. I still can't get my head round it but I obviously didn't check it on the night of the 8th – I think the intensity and difficulties of the situation I found myself in meant that I just wasn't functioning as I would normally. Unfortunately, the extra protection I had in place to prevent this kind of thing happening were, unbeknown to me, no longer in place. After receiving the phone call from the DCO in Monaco I tried to call Simon Thornton, but there was no answer. I later found out he had left his job three weeks earlier without anyone informing me; there were ten days when Simon would have spotted the inconsistency had he still been in place.

* * *

The weeks after that phone call were incredibly difficult. UKAD are permitted a period of two weeks to notify you of a whereabouts violation and during that time there is no strike against your name, so I was obliged to carry on racing for my team. I waited, praying a letter wouldn't arrive and that there had simply been a mistake in the system.

Therefore, five days after the phone call, I travelled from Ireland to the UK for the Aviva Women's Tour as planned. As a British world champion preparing for the Olympic games, it was very high pressure; every day I was put in front of the media. I hated it. Inside I was falling apart, waiting for the likely notification from UKAD, but I couldn't tell anybody. I was trying to answer questions about the Olympics, when I didn't even know if I would still be able to race. All the while I desperately wanted to be with my family. I won the Women's Tour because of my incredibly strong team, and thanks to the form that I had built up after months of hard work. The Monday after, I went for an easy bike ride to clear my mind; about an hour into it my phone rang. It was the UCI – they would be waiting outside my apartment until I returned to collect blood and urine samples. I raced home faster than my tired-out race legs wanted to go.

The letter from UKAD was hand-delivered when I was back home in Monaco after the tour, on the 13th night, the night of 22 June, in a blank envelope pushed under my apartment door. I watched from the couch as it was slid through. I still don't know why it wasn't sent recorded post or just put in my letterbox. It was like being in a movie; in fact during most of the events of that summer I felt like I was watching myself from a distance, on a rollercoaster that I couldn't get off.

* * *

In the two weeks while I was waiting for the notification letter I had already taken legal advice, so I had my appeal against the third strike ready and waiting, and as protocol dictates I submitted this to UKAD. This was rejected; it was then sent to an independent panel – a group of people drawn from sport – and it was rejected again. During this time I was still racing and I had not been suspended – I dropped out of the Giro D'Italia three days from the finish as a planned precautionary measure before the Olympics. At this point my training was severely compromised and the pressure of the strikes hanging over me was taking its toll, so I took the decision not to travel to Paris for La Course, which was a couple of weeks away on 24 July. No one seemed to know when I might receive a provisional suspension and my legal team were confident that I could successfully appeal it anyway. Once I had decided not to travel to La Course for my own reasons I had no more races scheduled between then and the Olympics, so my legal team let UKAD know and it was at this point that I received my provisional suspension. Due to the fact I wasn't racing anyway, we decided not to appeal the suspension to save precious time and resources to put towards the main appeals. Since no one knew I was suspended and La Course is such a high-profile race for my team and their sponsors, my team management only announced the decision to remove me from the starting line-up on the morning of the race – but in my mind I had withdrawn two weeks previously. It was incredibly surreal to be a suspended athlete and have that label – something I never dreamed would happen to me. But only now were we able to go to the Court of Arbitration in Sport to appeal all three strikes, including the Swedish 'strike'.

The CAS ruling over the Swedish 'strike' came down to two questions: UKAD had to prove that their DCO had done what was 'reasonable' in the circumstances to try to locate me. I had to prove that when the DCO had been unable to find me it was not down to the fact that I had been negligent in the way that I had made myself available for testing. I had to prove that I had been ready and waiting to be tested but UKAD had not tried hard enough to contact me. The final decision from CAS stated that, 'the panel, in examining all the circumstances of this unsuccessful attempt to test this athlete finds that the DCO did not comply with the WADA guidelines and, as such, did not do what was reasonable to try to locate Ms Armitstead.'

It goes on to say:

* * *

Specifically, the DCO reported in his Unsuccessful Attempt Report that he knew that Ms Armitstead was present at the hotel. He repeatedly tried to call her cell phone, which is one of the possible steps. There were other steps suggested by the WADA Guidelines which were reasonable under the circumstances that he did not undertake. He did not walk over to the team buses to see if there was anyone there who could help him, though there was uncontroverted evidence that at the time he was there the team mechanic was working within a few metres of the hotel doorway... He did not ask any of the people he saw in the breakfast room whether they knew how to locate someone from her cycling team. He did not make any real effort with the receptionist to see if in fact her room number could be located or indeed if the Boels-Dolmans team manager could be found and then he could locate Ms Armitstead. He could have made it clear his mission was important and all attempts needed to be made by the hotel staff to locate this athlete who clearly was staying at the hotel. All of these are reasonably basic and obvious steps he could easily have taken to prevent this unsuccessful attempt.

* * *

After the CAS hearing, I had a brief period of two days thinking, 'I am going to the Olympics', and it could become my sole focus again. I had a contractual obligation with the British Olympic Association to do a pre-Olympic press conference before the Games. It had been scheduled for the day before I flew but I would have done anything not to have had to do it under these circumstances. I was on the phone saying to the journalists that I had had a great build-up, that I was looking forward to the Olympics and so on – I felt like had to lie to every journalist who was there. For the last six weeks I had been involved in a confidential legal case and the Monday before my Olympic race was not the time to discuss it – that time, in my opinion, should have been later. It felt totally wrong. I felt like a fraud. I was in tears afterwards, saying to Phil, 'What on earth am I doing this for?' There is no time for strategic thinking because it's all happening so fast. It was a disaster.

The *Daily Mail* contacted Scott Dougal at British Cycling after the press conference and told him, 'We have this information. It's up to you how you deal with it.' To this day we do not know who leaked the story to them as there was only a select group who knew about my situation. I took up the opportunity to speak to them but I was in shock and it was impossible to get across the complexity of my case in one phone call.

The *Mail* printed their story late on 1 August; on 2 August I flew to Heathrow to catch my connection on to Rio. My darkest moment happened in the baggage claim after landing. Although Phil had been with me throughout most of the appeal period he had had to leave for a few days, which meant that as everything had unfolded in the media, I had had to deal with it on my own. The suitcases were delayed and as I was stood waiting for my bag, somebody walked over to me and said, 'I thought it was you', and then walked away. My tears were caught in my throat; I didn't want to give that person the satisfaction of seeing me cry. I walked away from the belt and went to a corner and cried. In that moment I felt so alone and helpless, I felt like a child and I really wanted my mum. I couldn't muster the strength to move. As an adult I had never felt like that; I was desperately sad. In the end I thought about my family and everything else going on in the world, and told myself, 'Stop being selfish and dramatic, get up and get on with it.' That is what I did, and it's what I have done ever since.

I was walking through Heathrow on the day the story broke, so I saw all the papers with my face on them. At a certain point, I stopped reading the press and so did my family. From our perspective, there were no balanced articles; there was no balanced approach or representation for me in the media. It was misreported over and over again, when what had happened was described as 'three missed tests' – the truth is it is one filing failure and one missed test, plus one alleged missed test, which was overruled. As a member of the public reading that headline, you would believe it, why wouldn't you? I had always assumed that the newspapers relayed full facts, but now I realise that is not the case, and that as an individual I feel that you have no way of stopping it unless you have endless resources to employ expensive lawyers.

So many of the stories implied that I might have been doping, which was scary because that wasn't the story. The story wasn't doping; I can see why people conflate the two, but there was no doping. I think I was a victim of my own success – 'Oh, that makes sense, that's why she won so much.' In that position you just have to take it. You can't reply to it or do anything. It was very difficult. In the beginning I did go and look at what was being said online. Later, things inevitably filtered back to me – people say things in conversations that they don't mean to, and you hear it. I had a really funny text from Beth, my friend at school. She said, 'Oh Lizzie, if only they knew that you had fallen out with me in Year 8 for six months because I smoked a cigarette.'

I was surprised by the abuse I received after the *Mail* story came out. It was partly the online comments, but also things like walking into a room and knowing that people are looking at you and saying, 'That's the girl who got three strikes.' Social media can be a horrible platform. It felt like people were getting pleasure from seeing me in a bad situation. It was personal. They were so angry with me. I understood that up to a point, but to be so vicious was something I didn't understand. It felt like a big wound turning into lots of little paper cuts.

I had never been bullied in my life and I didn't realise until then how lucky I was in that. I've been very fortunate. I've never been scared, or attacked for no reason. I'd never really appreciated what it was like to be on the receiving end; I've always thought, 'Well, why don't you stand up for yourself?' I've always been very confident: 'Well, why would you care what someone else thinks of you? Tell them to bugger off.'

But when it was so intense and overwhelming, I was in a position where I couldn't fight back at all. It definitely broke me down.

In the end I spoke to my father: 'Dad, I want to write my own statement, I don't want to do an interview with anybody.' So sitting in bed at 3am the night before my flight I wrote an account of what had happened and put it on Twitter. I've included it in the Appendix of this book.

I finally arrived in Rio.

There were paparazzi waiting for me when I landed; we had Mark Cavendish and Sir Bradley Wiggins with us, and there I was being ushered around a corner. I had security men with me all the time in Rio, two chaperones – I needed them. Two interviews had been set up for me, with Sky and the BBC. I thought, 'This is my opportunity to show people the human side of my story' and answer people's questions. I felt pressure to do myself justice.' But it was different. Normally, it's 'Hi Lizzie, how are you?' Off we go, but this was not the usual atmosphere, as if I was standing trial all over again. I was just shattered afterwards, because I'd pinned all my hopes on saying the right things, being able to express myself, and articulate what I felt, but I just couldn't find the right words and I felt myself becoming emotional. After that, I was even worse than I had been. I had not slept for days.

I had been training through all of this; in fact, I had trained really hard. That was the silver lining: I realised how much I love riding my bike, how much I rely on my bike. It's a place where I can think the best, where I can process things; it was my place. On my bike, I was not sitting around waiting; I was able to do something productive. The training had been done, and on the day of the Olympic road race I prepared as normal even though I was a bit of a zombie after the events of the previous week. The worst moment came on the start line: I looked to the left, saw my family and some journalists standing behind them; I hated it but I had to get on with the race.

I was happy Anna van der Breggen won the gold medal; she is a great Olympic champion and it wasn't my time. Early on, I had a puncture just as Emma Pooley was about to attack on the first climb. I looked down at my wheel and thought, 'Really?' There were no radios so there was no way Emma could be told. I kept my head on; I felt OK and I did what I could, but I didn't suffer. It sounds bizarre, but I didn't make it hurt on the climb the last time, not enough; I could have endured more but I don't think I truly wanted a medal. I did wonder what the point would be in winning. I love representing my country – I really feel pride in having the jersey on, because everyone is willing you to do well – but here I felt I was wearing a jersey that people didn't want me to wear. It wasn't as if I felt I was being willed on by the nation; I felt like I had bricks in my back. I wanted to race because I had earned the right to be there and I needed to do it for my family and friends and all those that had supported me. Pulling out of the race would almost have felt like an admission of guilt. I'd qualified the team, I'd put four years of work into it; mine and Phil's family had been to hell and back; I had to race for them. We had been through too much for me to give up at the last hurdle. But perhaps subconsciously I just didn't have the will to win any more.

*   *   *

On 11 November 2016, the Court of Arbitration in Sport ruled completely in my favour, meaning that UKAD became liable for my court costs and a proportion of my legal fees. UKAD had called for a full two-year ban and wanted me to cover all their legal fees, so had I lost I would have been bankrupt and banned. It was serious pressure. When I went to the Court, I had to hand over 23,000 Swiss francs that very morning for the room the appeal was held in. This is not something that you go into lightly. It's massive.

British Cycling appointed a legal team, who gave them initial legal advice that I was able to use, but after that I was on my own. If I had been an athlete who did not have the resources, I wouldn't have been able to afford to take the case to court and I would have been banned. I would have had no choice. If you haven't got the money, it's not even as if you have the time: you're given two weeks to come up with your defence.

At this time CAS wanted to make the award public, because of the interest in the case. I didn't want that because of the personal details surrounding my family circumstances contained within it. I owed it to Phil's family to not have this all brought to the media's attention again at such a difficult time for them

I am still very disappointed with UKAD as an organisation – at the time of writing they have yet to say, 'Yes, we made a mistake, we got it wrong.' They are supposed to protect clean athletes. I am a clean athlete and they more than anyone else should realise that, given how much I am tested compared to my competitors. It frustrates me that as individual athletes we are held to account, but as an organisation entirely devoted to the pursuit of clean sport they are not accountable when they make mistakes, as CAS found that they did in my case. Surely the organisation that is supposed to protect clean athletes and our sport should be as transparent as all of the athletes who fall under its administration?

CHAPTER 14

IT ISN'T ALWAYS ABOUT THE FINISH LINE

When I finished the road race in Rio there was no real sense of a page having been turned. It wasn't as if the finish line marked the end of the whole 'strikes' episode. It was still bubbling away. I had to stay in Rio for three days afterwards to do media and appearances, but I wanted to be out of there. I felt like I was trapped in this Olympic bubble. To add to this hemmed-in feeling, I felt more uncomfortable that we were living in luxury while there were kids walking around with no shoes on, and there was that guilty conscience that you have all the time if you go on holiday somewhere poorer. Had the Games gone well I'd probably have been a total hypocrite and it would have been lovely; I'd have just remembered the sandy beaches.

257

I can bring back vivid images of London 2012 in my mind; I can't do that with Rio. I couldn't tell you which sunglasses I was wearing in the race or what race number I had. I haven't looked at any photos from Rio. Because I'd had had such a negative experience of the Games, Rio felt all wrong and I desperately needed to escape. I was in a dark place when I was there.

I came home and went back to Otley for a couple of days. I didn't need to ride my bike, Phil was there and we just did what we wanted, which was nice. The Olympic Games were still going on but not in our family. Straight away, I travelled to Sweden to race; I was grateful for that and I was grateful too for my friendship with Evelyn Stevens, my teammate, half a dozen years older than me and heading for retirement after a season in which she had taken the world hour record and won three stages in the Giro d'Italia. I knew how much she wanted to win the world team time trial, her last race, and that was what kept me going; it was the only thing I could train for. That was the only thing I could motivate myself for – not to let my teammates down – and it made me realise that in training there is a difference between training and suffering. To win you have to suffer so much; I just didn't have the ability to go that deep in training. I did what I needed to but that extra bit of sparkle wasn't there. I couldn't find it, but my condition, my professionalism and my conscientiousness took me through. I ended up in good enough form for the

Worlds, where I would try to defend my rainbow jersey in the road race.

The media's fascination with the 'strikes' thankfully seemed to die down when the Rio road race was over, but in September, the Fancy Bears' leaks of Therapeutic Use Exemptions (TUE) got going, including the revelation that Sir Bradley Wiggins had had a cortisone injection before winning the Tour de France, the media spotlight returned to questioning British cyclists. It felt so sad; it was unfair on all the riders who'd had success – the Great Britain track-cycling team – because it wasn't fair that any doubt was cast and it hung over me that my story contributed to that in any way, though ironically I have never had a TUE in my career. I felt there was irresponsible reporting of the Fancy Bears' story – there was a headline that Emma Johannson had had a TUE, but it was for an operation. It was a non-story that shouldn't have been written about and shouldn't have been a big headline.

It had all seemed to settle down coming up to the Worlds, but the fear of speaking to the press again made me very anxious. Unfortunately, the events of the summer definitely affects the way I feel about the media. If I'm honest, I don't like doing interviews and media; I like winning and I like bike racing. My whole experience has made me question this aspect of my job as a modern sportsperson: Can't you just ride your bike and win, do the interviews after the race and then go home and not talk to anybody? But cycling relies on fans, sponsors, investment, so as a female world champion, in the position I was in, I had to do it.

Once in Qatar for Worlds, the preparations with the Boels-Dolmans team went perfectly and after a three-year campaign and countless training camps prior to the road race, we won the World Team Time Trial championship. I couldn't have been prouder – it was the perfect swansong for Evie and amazing to be part of. About four people turned up at the press conference; every question was directed at me, about Wiggins. It was so disappointing when I was sat there with a winning team – four women who I respected and admired – so I felt confident enough to say, 'I'm not answering that question, these women deserve to be in the spotlight', which they did. Those riders had had an amazing season but people wanted to hijack the press conference to ask about Wiggins; again, I felt guilty about that.

Somewhere among all that, two things happened: Yorkshire was awarded the world road race championship for 2019. I am a very proud Yorkshirewoman; there is a rich heritage of cycling in our region and I have no doubts that our community of countless racers, volunteers, race organisers and amateur cyclists will make the World Championships a success like no other I will experience in my career. The prospect of a home World Championships is so exciting, the atmosphere on course will be phenomenal and reflect our country's pride and enthusiasm for a sport which was so much smaller ten years ago when I first started riding my bike in Yorkshire.

Meanwhile, I also came fourth in a blisteringly hot road race: the main tactic of the GB road team was centred on hydration: 'drink enough and it's anybody's race'. I had gone into the race happy to play a shadowing role and preserve my energies for an inevitable sprint, while the rest of the team was given the freedom to ride for themselves. Given my lack of motivation and focus going into the race it wasn't fair, despite being defending champion, to ask for a full team to work for me. I sprinted to fourth, a very respectable finish in a pure sprinters' race. I was the only rider to finish inside the top five in both the Olympics and World Championships in 2016. I am incredibly proud of that as at so many moments it would have been easy to give up.

*　*　*

In cycling terms, that brought 2016 to an end. I will remember that summer as one of the worst periods of my life, but also as one of the best. I experienced a trauma that I never expected to find myself in the middle of, but I survived it and I married Phil. The first will be remembered as a blip in the greater scheme of things, but the latter will keep me happy for the rest of my life. Maintaining some measure of perspective was one of the only things that got me through that summer, along with lots of people who showed kindness and compassion – rowers in the hotel in Rio, a security guard, air hostesses, the local community in Otley. I had some great support, people who took time, asked me questions, and once they understood the story they had a totally different perspective.

Phil and I had planned our wedding for September 2016, between the Olympics and the World Road Race Championships. When you get married, people feel free to give you all sorts of opinions, but it is another case of having to have confidence in your own reasoning. To me, a wedding day is important, but I was not going to pile pressure on it by trying to make it the biggest day of my life. I was more excited by the fact of marriage, of being married to Phil.

It is unusual for professional cyclists to get married before the end of the cycling season, but there were various reasons for choosing our date. The wedding was very family-centred; we wanted as many of our family to be there as possible and we wanted to have the best chance of Phil's dad being at the wedding. As a result, the date suited our family and friends rather than the racing calendar. If we had waited until the season was over, the honeymoon would have been short because we would both have had to start training for 2017. The target for the year was the Olympics rather than the world championship, although it was important for me to be at the race to show respect for the race and the next potential champion. The flight for our honeymoon was booked for the day after the finish of the Worlds.

My mum had said she would organise the wedding – she is the planner in the family. I bought a dress and fixed a hen do, although that wasn't easy: there was one free weekend in the entire year. My plan was to turn up on the day, put the dress on and say my vows. I felt immensely laid back about it; it was not going to be a traditional formal wedding. We booked the church where my parents had tied the knot 36 years earlier and we had the reception in the Cavendish Pavilion cafe by the river on the Bolton Abbey estate – it's somewhere I've ridden to and spent time as a child. We knew we wouldn't get married in a hotel: Phil and I see quite enough of those during the season.

I had to be fairly steadfast about the whole plan. I wanted six bridesmaids, but I didn't have the time or the inclination to go out and find them identical dresses. They were each provided with a budget and told to use it to get a green dress. It's not obvious to get your head around if you have a traditional view that weddings are something that should take up hours of planning, but all I wanted was for them to look good and feel happy, and just wearing green was enough. I don't think a wedding is about spending thousands of pounds on one day: I'd rather spend it on other experiences.

There was one false note at the wedding: a newspaper called the church secretary, who is an old lady, and coaxed her into giving away all the details, what time it started and so on, the ceremony; and the minister told us that she was upset when she realised what she'd done. That was a sad thing because she just felt so guilty and it was not necessary.

We had a deal with *OK!* magazine that had been set up before Rio – it's not really me to be honest, and especially after everything that had happened I wanted our day to remain private – but it's a financial decision and we weren't in a position to turn down the money to pay for our wedding. They weren't there – we just sold the photos for a fee. On the day, when there were paparazzi outside the church anyway, I was happy that we had sold the pictures in our way, especially as various photos ended up in the papers anyway.

It was very important to me that it wasn't a formal wedding, so we got married in the church I grew up with; Phil's priest came over from Ireland which meant we acknowledged both religions and kept everybody happy. Phil and I went off to a field with a nice view to have our pictures taken because I didn't want anything too staged. At the reception we had a Sunday roast dinner with speeches and then went for a ride on the Bolton Abbey steam train. It was the perfect day, the sun was shining, it was wonderful to be surrounded by the people we cared. about In the end Gerry, Phil's father; couldn't come over from Ireland though, which was hard – we definitely felt he was missing – but apart from that it was everything we wanted.

I thought long and hard about whether I should change my name and the positive and negatives of both options, and in the end it wasn't a political decision, it was a personal choice that I wanted to be a family, to be one of the Deignans. I didn't want to be an Armitstead-Deignan. If I was going to do it I was going to change my passport the next day. I went against advice – people said I should remain Lizzie Armitstead: 'You are a brand, don't do it, it will cost you financially.' Changing my name was absolutely not a re-branding exercise; in fact, it was probably a reaction against the whole idea that I should care about being a brand. It was about me and Phil getting married, and our relationship will outlive my cycling career.

*　*　*

Looking back at the summer of 2016, I learnt a great deal. What I went through has taught me to be less judgemental. I have always been black and white – now I'm less so. I used to get frustrated by teammates getting upset in team meetings and think it was unprofessional, but I like to think I'd be more understanding of people having things going on in their lives that affect their work now. I've become far more conscious that behind closed doors people are going through all kinds of hardship that we can't understand.

My mum said she was sad that I had had to learn lessons so early in life about things she hoped would come later for me. I have begun to worry less about the little things in life and sometimes feel ashamed at feeling sorry for myself.

There are bigger issues in the world than my personal story: I know I am one of the lucky ones.

Until October 2015 I didn't really see 'whereabouts' as an overwhelming feature of my job. It was something I did with apparent ease; it didn't have any effect on my sleep or planning – I just did it. Then that all changed. Was it subconscious arrogance at being a clean British athlete that meant I felt the WADA system was there for 'others' and that I didn't need to take it as seriously as I do now? It's impossible to say.

Now, I update my room number every time I go into a hotel, even though it's not a requirement of the system, but as a failsafe – however, it's not always that simple. In Sweden this year, at my first race after the Olympics, I received an email from my new contact at British Cycling, saying, 'Hi, Lizzie can you update your whereabouts to include your room number?' I replied, 'I have done.' 'Well it's not on the system.' So I took a screenshot of it with my phone, and my BC contact screenshot it off her computer, and my room number wasn't showing up on the computer. You are left thinking 'How?' You wonder just how well the whereabouts app on the phone works, and after Fancy Bears you wonder how accessible it is to others.

'If she was called Armitscked then she would be banned'. I can understand how people get carried away; they read the news on Russia and somehow marry my story and the story of Putin and his government-led doping scheme. But I'm Lizzie Armitstead from Otley and I don't belong in the same conversation as the Russian dopers. Equally, I believe if I had come from some other nation then they would have celebrated the fact that I was cleared to ride the Olympics and that nation would have supported me. Take Italian cyclist Diego Rosa, who had an alleged third strike overturned by CAS the same week as me – he cycled at the Olympics with no scrutiny hanging over him. I have subsequently had any number of GB Olympians telling me that they went to Rio on two strikes and of another high-profile British sportsperson who recently had an alleged third strike overturned by CAS. It is more common than you might believe, which makes me question the system, but I don't have a solution.

'She's lucky she got away with it because she is world champion'; 'it should be the same rules for everybody'. The truth is that being a world champion had nothing to do with me winning that case. I can categorically say the rules are not the same for everybody, but I most certainly don't fall on the lenient side. I am one of the most scrutinised female athletes in Britain and internationally; the standards are far from universal. I was discussing it with a teammate and explained that I have to update my whereabouts three months in advance; so does she – but then she never logs-in again, she simply emails her national anti-doping agency when she has a change of hotel. She doesn't have to change anything on the computer system herself. Her view was that if there were spot checks, she'd absolutely have been banned, but she's never encountered them in her career. If you look at the number of women in the testing pool, it's a bigger number now but certainly doesn't include everyone. Only in June 2016 during the women's Tour did a number of other, high- profile, riders receive emails to say they were being added to the system that I've been on since I was 18 years old. My team is now sponsored by a teaching hospital in Netherlands, so we had a meeting with a team doctor in which he explained the blood passport to us, a system designed to look for changes or anomalies in blood values to highlight doping. The system relies on trends spotted over a period of time from a series of sample collections. He asked everyone in the room how many samples they had in their blood passport. I have a blood passport dating back throughout my career; there were riders in the room who had no passport at all.

The system needs to be strict, given what has gone on in the past, with riders avoiding the testers in various ways, but it also needs to be equitable and it needs to be operated in a very professional way. There are prominent riders within cycling from other nations who are not on the same system, or are not even on whereabouts at all. Going into the Worlds I knew that people I was racing against weren't under the same pressure, and it was the same going to Rio. The implications are immense: if you don't put down your every movement that could cost you your entire reputation and with it your livelihood. That means that the system has to be operated in a very professional way.

* * *

The details of my wedding said something about me: my character and the way I am stem more from my family, my friends and where I come from than from my cycling. My upbringing and the people around me are what have allowed me to be who I am: for example, my sister's confidence and balance in her approach to life have been an inspiration

Cycling has been my job for my entire adult life. I left school at 18 and moved to Manchester to join the British Cycling academy. Riding a bike has never been a hobby for me, so it is not a pastime that has turned into a way of making money. If anything, I am fortunate that over the years it has developed into a passion.

Curious as this might sound, I enjoy riding my bike more now than I did when I was in my teens. To start with, I found it a bit alien, a bit weird. I didn't really understand it. There was huge pressure around it as well, and in the track environment it didn't always feel that different from being at school – I came across that teacher–student relationship that I didn't like. Now, on the very rare occasions when I get to ride my bike solely for fun, I love it. After a major win, when I have achieved a big goal, I will go out for a coffee spin with friends and allow myself two or three days when I don't take it seriously, purely in order to maintain some balance. I ride my bike in the off-season, and even if it's just a city bike rented in London, I enjoy being outside. I like what it gives you: independence, speed, fresh air.

As for what drives me to train and race, it's complicated.

I like suffering. That sounds odd, but it is a tangible thing. There is a straightforward formula: the more you hurt, the better you become. I feel my body is an apparatus, a machine that needs driving hard in order to be at its best. I could be addicted to exercise – I think it must be the endorphins. I struggle to switch off when I'm on holiday. I worry about retirement. I need physical activity: when I don't have it, I'm not the best person to be around.

I'm not motivated by the numbers I hit in training, about whether I managed a bigger power output this week than last. What I relish is more general than that: the constant push ahead, seeing what I am capable of. That is what I find makes my job rewarding: constant, tangible improvement alongside balancing this with fatigue and finding the limits of your own mind and body.

I can trace that love of activity back to where it began: as a family we spent so much time outside; we were always out in the fresh air. I didn't like our family Sunday walks as a family, but you could say that my father got his way in the end and I became an out-of-doors person.

The summer of 2016 made me realise that I love riding my bike even more than I thought I did, and it made me aware of the reasons I'm doing it. I love bike racing, the actual race; it's like chess, the focus you have, the fact it's controllable, it's fun. There is nothing else like it. I'm just really good at it and you like things you're good at.

As a sportsperson the retirement question is always a

difficult one. I want to race as long as I can be one of the world's best. The list of targets can be endless, I am not sure if I will achieve them all, but I just hope that when it comes my retirement will be my own decision and not forced upon me by injury or other external factors. I wondered about retiring at the end of 2016, but I'm enjoying it too much to stop.

There is another deadline that will dictate the end of my cycling career. I have always wanted children, and I have always wanted a lot of them.

I couldn't contemplate coming back to cycling full-time as a mother. I hugely admire Jess Ennis-Hill, or in cycling terms Paralympic gold medallist Sarah Storey, for competing at the highest level again after having a baby, but I just don't think that is possible in my case. As a road cyclist, I am travelling for at least 200 days a year, and personally couldn't contemplate that alongside the responsibility of being a mum. At the moment, it seems likely we will ultimately return to Yorkshire to live in a house we have been restoring. In that period of our lives it will be good to have our family close to us.

I've missed my Olympic goal in Rio, but there will be other targets to focus on. I have to hope that women's cycling will keep moving forward and that there will be new races to target. In 2017, Liège–Bastogne–Liège and Amstel Gold Race, to name just two, and I would like to win Flèche Wallonne, and other races that don't suit me on paper. My goals are always personal. I wanted to win the Tour of

Flanders, but not because it is a high profile event. I just wanted to win Flanders because I love that race.

No matter what you win, the media are constantly looking forward to the next thing. No sooner had I crossed the line in Flanders than I was asked what my next goal was. As an athlete it is very important to be focused on your own ambitions and not lose sight of your own targets. I have found blocking out others expectations, or in some cases advice, has been a hugely successful part of my mental focus. Repeating victories has never motivated me; I am always searching for a new dream.

Cycling came to me at a perfect time in my life because I had no idea what I was going to do when I left school. I wasn't passionate about anything in particular, but I loved sport, and I thought, 'Right, this is something I can be good at.' There are crossroads moments in your life and one of them came on that day when British Cycling visited my school, but it was down to me to seize that chance.

Often, you are only going to get one opportunity. So it frustrates me when people hold themselves back from doing things due to fear of what people might think of them. I think it was my grandma who said to me, 'Don't worry about what people are thinking when they look at you, because they are more worried about themselves.' In a social situation, no one is looking at what I am wearing and judging me; people are too often thinking that they themselves are being judged. When my brother let go of his hang-ups about road cycling, it opened up a whole new world to him. He could have gone through life not having got to race on the road because he thought downhill mountain biking was more cool. I do care about whether the people I care about respect me and love me, but in the greater scheme of things you can waste so much energy worrying about other people. My priority in life will always be my husband, my family and friends. Good relationships with them will always be more rewarding than any victory.

If there is a message in my story, it is that you should concentrate on what makes you happy, finding the confidence to strive for that, rather than doing what society tells you to do. You can't please everybody; accepting that is the way to fulfilment. It is about being the best version of yourself that you can manage, and having the confidence to refuse to let your light be dimmed by social pressure or the environment that you end up in. I feel that I flourished at every stage in my life when I took control, be that leaving the track, spending time being single or writing this book. That in turn enabled me to be happy, and being secure in myself enabled the people around me to be happy.

I'm sometimes asked what I would say to someone wanting to be the next Lizzie Deignan. In sporting terms, the advice is simple: say yes to opportunities. Push yourself out of your comfort zone. Don't take no for an answer. But the genuine answer in the broader sense is: you shouldn't want to be the next Lizzie Deignan. There is only one of each of us. Celebrate your uniqueness and don't let a lack of confidence hold you back.

APPENDIX

The following message was posted on my Twitter page on 3rd August 2016.

I am writing this statement in my own words, something I have wanted to do from the very beginning. Understandably people have questions which I want to answer as openly and honestly as I can. I hope people understand that speaking with journalists is a necessary part of my job, speaking directly to the public in a statement like this, which has not been ghost written or moulded by somebody else is unheard of. I want to take responsibility for this message. This is my life and not a game of headlines. I want to state the facts but also try to explain my situation further. I believe I owe this statement to sports fans, people who love sport like I do.

As an 18-year-old schoolgirl I was introduced to the whereabouts system 9 years ago. Since then the system has evolved and developed, post-October 2015 I recognised this and requested further education from UKAD. I will come back to this later.

By submitting my whereabouts I am consenting to people coming into my house or hotel and taking blood and urine samples. This is a part of my sport that I accept and whole heartedly support.

LIZZIE ARMITSTEAD

To add some background before I explain the specific details of my 3 'strikes':

I have been tested 16 times in 2016.

I have a clear and valid blood passport (a more detailed use of looking for doping violations by looking for trends vs anomalies in my blood values)

I have been tested after every victory this season.

I am on the road for around 250 days a year, with around 60 race days.

I have never tested positive for a banned substance.

I have never taken a banned substance.

I will present the facts of my 3 'strikes':

Sweden 20th August 2015:

UKAD are allowed a maximum of two weeks to inform you of a 'strike'. When I received the letter from UKAD I immediately contested it with a written explanation, this was not accepted on the eve of me travelling to America for my world championships. I had no legal advice or external support at the time.

Last week:

CAS ruled quickly and unanimously in my favour and cleared me of any wrongdoing, because:

I was at the hotel I stated.

The DCO didn't do what was reasonable or necessary to find me.

I was tested the next day; this test was negative.

Calling an athlete's mobile phone is not a method approved by UKAD to try and locate an athlete, as such it is not an argument against me that I slept with my phone on silent in order not to disturb a room mate.

Put simply I was available and willing to provide a sample for UKAD.

2nd 'strike' October 2015:

Despite being reported as a 'missed test' this was in fact a 'filing failure'.

UKAD did not try to test me; instead this was an administrative spot check. They found an inconsistency between an overnight accommodation and a morning time slot.

APPENDIX

A busy post-World Championship period meant I had no firm plans and as such was changing address and plans very quickly. I made a mistake. This was an honest mistake rather than trying to deceive anybody. A mistake that many athletes who are honest with themselves will admit to having made themselves. I was tested by UKAD later that week and produced a negative result.

In December 2015 I met with UKAD and British cycling to discuss a support plan in order to avoid a 3rd potential 'strike'.

Simon Thornton from British Cycling was put in place to check my whereabouts on a bi-weekly basis. We had regular contact and he would help me with any problems, effectively he was a fail safe mechanism. Since meeting with UKAD my whereabouts updates have been as detailed and specific as they can possibly be. Going as far as I can in describing my locations to avoid any further issues.

Unfortunately this system fell apart on the 9th June when UKAD tried to test me in my hour slot and I was not where I had stated I would be. Simon Thornton had left British Cycling three weeks prior to my strike without anybody informing me. We worked under a policy of 'no news was good news' as outlined in my support plan with UKAD. If Simon was still in place the following oversight could have been prevented. My overnight accommodation (the bed in which I was sleeping the morning of the test) was correct, but I had failed to change the one hour testing slot, it was clearly impossible to be in both locations.

This is where I believe I have the right to privacy. My personal family circumstances at the time of the test were incredibly difficult, the medical evidence provided in my case was not contested by UKAD; they accepted the circumstances I was in. UKAD did not perceive my situation to be 'extreme' enough to alleviate me of a negligence charge. A psychiatrist assessment of my state of mind at the time was contrary. In my defence I was dealing with an emergency family situation and it was a traumatic time and I forgot to change a box on a form. I am not a robot, I am a member of a family, my commitment to them comes over and above my commitment to cycling. This will not change and as a result I will not discuss this further, our suffering does not need to be part of a public trial. I hope I have made it clear that family comes before cycling, I am not obsessively driven to success in cycling, I love my sport, but I would never cheat for it.

To conclude:

I currently have 1 filing failure and 1 missed test.

The reason this hasn't been discussed publicly until now is because I had the right to a fair trial at CAS, it is clear sensationalised headlines have a detrimental effect to any legal case.

In the days following the revelations in the press my family and I have been the victim of some incredibly painful comments. I ask people to take a moment to put themselves in my shoes; I am an athlete trying to do my best; I am a clean athlete. I am the female Road Race World Champion; I operate in a completely different environment to the majority of athletes in the testing pool. I am self coached. I race for a Dutch women's team, away from the British cycling set up, which doesn't have a budget to match a world tour men's team who have staff specifically in place to support riders with whereabouts. I don't wish to make excuses; I made one mistake, which was noticed in a 'spot check'; my second strike came at a time when anybody who lives for and loves their family would understand my oversight. It's as simple as ticking the wrong box on a form.

I love sport and the values it represents, it hurts me to consider anybody questioning my performances. Integrity is something I strive for in every part of my life. I will hold my head high in Rio and do my best for Great Britain, I am sorry for causing anyone to lose faith in sport, I am an example of what hard work and dedication can achieve. I hate dopers and what they have done to sport.

To any of the 'Twitter army' reading this, do yourself a favour and go for a bike ride. It's the most beautiful thing you can do to clear your mind.

ACKNOWLEDGEMENTS

Phil

Thank you for being everything I hoped for and more in a husband. Meeting you and learning that we share the same values and dreams, on top of your big blue eyes and Donegal accent, meant you had me hooked from our first date. Falling in love with someone that you admire and respect is something that I will never take for granted. Thank you for believing in me and always pushing me to be confident and stand up for myself. With your support I feel so much stronger in every situation; you are absolutely my better half and I am so excited to share our lives together.

My family

Mum – a woman of so many talents and a big warm heart. You make me laugh almost daily. Thank you for always having an open mind and encouraging me to go for it in life. I couldn't have hoped for a better female role model to guide me; your constant energy levels and enthusiasm are an inspiration!

Dad – when it comes to almost every question in life I look to you for an answer. Thank you for always having an answer or helping me to find it. Your relationship with Mum has given me such a strong foundation to build my life on; I admire you as a role model as a husband and father to our family. I have inherited your passion for the outdoors and I'm grateful for your introduction.

Kate, my big sister – thank you for being a friend as well as a sister. I look to you for guidance on almost everything and you always seem to know the right thing to do. You have encouraged me to be brave and proud of who I am. I look forward to our days together when I don't have to consider a bike ride interfering with our plans!

Nick, my big brother – you are one of the most entertaining people I know and you always have an alternative viewpoint. We have shared a lot of memories together – on and off the bike – and when cycling is getting too much I often think back to them and laugh. Thank you for being a great friend.

Grandma and Grandad – I don't know many grandparents who have travelled as far and wide as you two to support their grandchild. You manage to support all of your 16 grandchildren with the same level of commitment and love; you are simply brilliant and I love you both very much.

The 'Armitsteads' and the 'Dunns'. I am incredibly lucky

to have such a big, loving and warm family on both sides; thank you for being a constant reminder that family will always be the most important part of my life.

Friends

Beth – my oldest friend. You have my back. You keep my feet well and truly on the ground, and having a friend like you is so valuable in my ever-changing world. Thank you.

The 'boys' – thank you for reminding me that cycling is a small world and the biggest sport in the world is actually Rugby League. If I need a good laugh I always look to you.

Pippa – I don't know what I would have done without you through some of the hard times. Your energy and enthusiasm for life are sometimes hard to keep up with, but I appreciate you always reminding me that there is more to life than sport.

Tiff – we are so different, yet we have such a strong friendship. It's so nice to have a friend that understands the demands of my job but has a completely different outlook on life. Our training rides have helped me achieve my dreams – thank you.

Cycling

Emma Wade – I can't imagine that being my agent is always easy. You are a constant element of trust and control in my team. I would not have managed my career as successfully without you by my side. I think our relationship stands for loyalty and integrity in an industry that doesn't always lend itself to that.

Danny Stam – my manager and friend. We have been through so many ups and downs together. Thank you for always believing in me and giving me strength when I felt like giving up. We clicked almost immediately, you have made all the races and road trips together successful, but most of all a lot of fun. We could write a second book just from our adventures!

Phil West – without you I would have been lost. Thank you for setting me up in cycling with such patience and care. I learnt how to race from you; I learnt to believe in myself because of you. We will remain friends long after I disappear from the limelight.

Anna Blyth – living in Fallowfield through the highs and lows of both of our careers was made so much more bearable by living with you. Having a teammate that was also an honest friend who made me laugh every day was integral to my motivation through those hard winter months. Like your classic bottle-green mini, they don't make them like you any more.

Joanna Rowsell Shand – I am so grateful that throughout my whole career you have been there right alongside me. I am so very proud of you, on and off the bike!

Boels and Dolmans – my team for six years. Thank you for your enthusiasm and support for womens cycling. From a club team to the best team in the world. We can all be so proud of our journey.

Teammates and support

Christine Majerus – integral to so many of my victories.

Evelyn Stevens – hilarious conversations that kept me laughing through many races and training camps.

Marieke Van Wanroij – the kindest most generous bike rider I ever had the pleasure of riding with.

Michel – we communicate via body language, but Michel understands how I work and with a simple hug can make things better.

Smiley – you brought a smile and enthusiasm to our team that we needed, you were the missing piece of our now dominant team.

JC – the best massage money can buy and a fantastic French teacher.

Ivano – motopacing is the best kind of training but with an Italian driving and buying the coffee afterwards it is even more productive!

Miss Kendall – Proof that if you are lucky enough to get a good teacher they can help shape your future, thank you for your encouragement in all aspects of my development at school.

Thank you to Joel, Matt, Lizzie and everyone at Blink for your patience and understanding while working on this book. Thank you to William Fotheringham; it was a pleasure to write my book with you and I am grateful to you for being so forthright that I had a story worth sharing

I'd also like to thank all of the people who have supported me throughout my career and that have enabled me to get where I am – from fans and my team around me to all of the sponsors I have worked with. Forgive me if I have forgotten everyone but this includes: Adidas, BP, Cycleplan, Wattbike, Oakley, Specialized, Hornby, Kellogg's, Garmin-Cervélo, Boels-Dolmans and many more.

Finally, thank you to everybody who has taken the time to read my story and to support my career. I am always humbled by the amount of support given to me by the public. I appreciate that my sport relies on so many people to make it a success: volunteers, race organisers, fans, sponsors and fellow competitors. Thank you to all those who have played any part in my career; it's impossible to recognise you all here, but I hope you understand how much I treasure it and understand that without it, I and cycling in this country wouldn't be in the position we are now.